Rajasthan
THE PAINTED WALLS
OF SHEKHAVATI

Ganesha, the elephant-headed
God of the Portal who is
believed to remove obstacles.
Here he is painted above a door
in the *Soné Chandi Ki haveli*,
'the house of gold and silver',
built at Mahensar in 1846 by
Sej Ram Podar.

FRANCIS WACZIARG & AMAN NATH

Rajasthan
THE PAINTED WALLS
OF SHEKHAVATI

CROOM HELM LONDON

First published 1982
© BLA Publishing Limited/Francis Wacziarg/Aman Nath
1982

Colour origination by Chris Willcock Reproductions
Photoset by Southern Positives and Negatives (SPAN),
  Lingfield, Surrey
Printed in Spain by Heraclio Fournier SA

This book was designed and produced by
BLA Publishing Limited, Lingfield, Surrey

CROOM HELM LTD
2–10 St John's Road, London SW11

ISBN 0–7099–2762–2

Contents

The sand of the desert
is not from the hourglass.
It slips through time's fingers
unrecorded. And in this timelessness
dunes migrate
escaping the measure of clocks.

But man continues
to make his own history,
dotting the sand with his landmarks,
etching his dates on the desert.

AMAN NATH

To our parents who taught us
the joys of wandering.

Foreword

INDIA'S CORNUCOPIA OF ART continues to reveal happy surprises. This small, bright volume invites us to view little-known wall paintings from an area not often visited either by tourists or by 'Indologists'. Unlike most books on Indian art, which reconsider the ancient glories of Ajanta, Ellora, and the Taj Mahal, this one brings us closer to current Indian life through the comparatively recent murals of the *havelis*, or mansions, which are part of a barely extinct art once patronized by families some of whom remain India's leading merchants and bankers. Although the more active members of these business dynasties now spend most of each year in Bombay, New Delhi or Calcutta, they have still kept their ancestral homes, each of which contains the family shrine as well as memorabilia.

Inasmuch as art hisorians usually concentrate upon acknowledged 'masterpieces', the peaks of their traditions, or explore 'primitive' and folkloristic culture, the middling area of the mercantile world is frequently overlooked, especially in India. A balanced aesthetic 'diet', however, cannot be limited to the sublimity of the Classics and the earthier spirituality of the finest folk-songs or bronzes. The *haveli* paintings fall between the two poles. Their artists considered themselves craftsmen, and they were probably paid according to the area covered, the quality of materials and the complexity of the subjects. Professionals, who took pride in their work, they usually belonged to artisan families, whose fortunes depended upon the local economy as well as their talent. At best, some of them moved from the bazaars and found patronage at

Self-portrait of a fresco painter in the Satya Narain temple, built in 1911 at Dundlod. His painting of the legend of Dhola and Maru in the same temple (far right) has now been whitewashed over.

Rajput courts, where artists were maintained along with carpenters, chefs, armourers and many other artisans. Occasionally a Rajput prince doted on painting and encouraged his artists with generosity, devotion and imagination. Such patrons vied with one another in finding and hiring artists of genius.

Often Muslim *ustads*, or masters, worked for Hindu employers and vice versa; and they were not averse to painting Hindu subjects. Occasionally one or two of their sons were fortunate and talented enough to be trained and kept on in the royal atelier. Others were likely to revert to the bazaar workshop, where they were assisted by the 'trade secrets' of the family, techniques and motifs passed on from generation to generation as a valuable legacy. Some of the pictures reproduced here, such as that of the lovers Dhola and Maru hurtling across the desert on their camel, are stock subjects found in virtually all schools of Rajput painting. Among the tracings, sketches and partially coloured miniatures stored in bundles by artist families one could expect to find several versions of this popular theme.

The mood of the *haveli* murals is that of brass bands playing marches, of festive parades, or of decorously cheerful family weddings and reunions. Much of the appeal is nostalgic, evocative of almost forgotten celebrations brought to mind by flowers pressed in old books, or by dog-eared, faded photographs. Especially appealing to us is the open-eyed innocence of the painters, so apparent in their work. Joyously, and without a trace of envy, they shared their patrons' pride of position and possession. They were deeply moved by vicarious delight, and their pictures, now mellowed by time's patination, pass this on to us.

These paintings, indoor and out, were in progress over long stretches of time; and to the families for whom they were created, they must revive a multiplicity of stirring memories. When old Auntie So-and-so wanders through the richly adorned public rooms, or views the façades, she must be reminded of colourful marriage and birth celebrations, associated with dozens of loved – or at least tolerated – relatives, in addition to servants and family friends. For these great houses were built in keeping with the Indian joint family system, in which children, parents, grandparents, aunts, uncles, and cousins all occupy a single complex, sometimes, as in these *havelis*, with shared as well as private apartments. If she is truly venerable, she might remember the circumstances behind the appropriately black portrayal of Victoria, the Queen-Empress, based upon the official mourning portrait by Sir Hubert von Herkomer, in which the Queen's tears well in recollection of the Prince Consort. Based upon an English steel-engraving (acquired during trade with the English or given by the British Resident), this prophetically Picassoid rendering marked the patron as a loyal subject of the Raj, and the artist as one of the many anonymous Indian painters who intuitively was far ahead of his times.

A flying car at Fatehpur.

The Jalan *haveli* in Fatehpur with its fresco of a European wedding.

Two cars from Ramgarh.

It is difficult to escape the mark of the Raj in these wall paintings, many of which were created at the time of the Coronation Durbar of 1911, when those true to the Crown spruced up much of India in honour of the visit of King George V and Queen Mary. Even awesome Shiva has been Anglicised, and bicycles, trains and motor cars proclaim their nation of origin. We particularly enjoy the long, black, insect-like touring car, with its smart chauffeur and stately occupants, one of whom wears a solar topi. Presumably, its depiction was inspired by a grand and up-to-date family extravagance which provided further means of sharing pride in prosperity with friends and mere passers-by.

One wonders if the *haveli* muralists represented here ever saw a railway train. If they did, they evidently preferred to trace and enlarge from a woodcut one of the tidal wave of popular graphic ephemera turned out in nineteenth-century India, and now mostly lost or destroyed. As can be seen from the tidily symmetrical and formulaic compositions, in which wheels, passengers, and smoke was filtered and rearranged according to ancient ideals.

Sadly, the wall paintings in this book may not long survive. In traditional India damaged images have lost their sanctity and power, and broken or eroded objects are usually discarded as worthless. Moreover, traditional artists, such as those responsible for these murals, are a dying breed, challenged in the nineteenth century by photography, and later by mass-production printing. Although a few painters live on and find occasional employment in connection with weddings, when they might be called upon to depict the bridegroom swooping through the skies in an aeroplane, they cannot survive for more than a decade or so. Happily, Messrs Wacziarg and Nath have recorded an excellent selection of their work for *haveli* façades, which are joyous as wedding sweets and still hint at the lavish hospitality within.

A railway train from Ramgarh.

STUART CARY WELCH
Senior Lecturer in Fine Arts,
Harvard University
Special Consultant and Head of the
Department of Islamic Art,
The Metropolitan Museum of Art

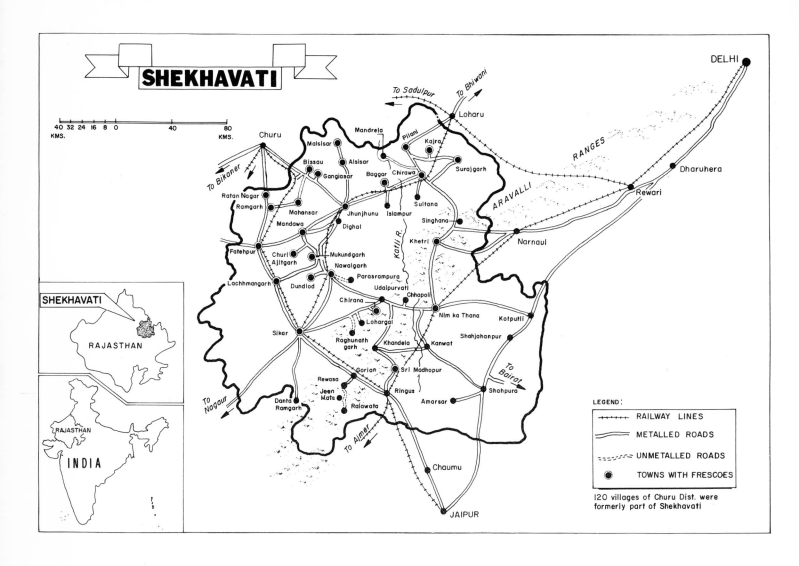

SHEKHAVATI

DELHI

To Sadulpur
To Bhiwani
Loharu
Mandrela
Pilani
Kajra
Malsisar
Churu
Bissau
Alsisar
Gangiasar
Baggar
Chirawa
Surajgarh
Ratan Nagar
Ramgarh
Mahansar
Jhunjhunu
Islampur
Sultana
Mandawa
Dighal
Singhana
Fatehpur
Churi
Ajitgarh
Mukundgarh
Nawalgarh
Khetri
Lachhmangarh
Dundlod
Parasrampura
Udaipurvati
Chhapoli
Chirana
Nim ka Thana
Kotputli
Lohargal
Shahjahanpur
Sikar
Raghunath garh
Khandela
Kanwat
Gorian
Sri Madhopur
Rewasa
Jeen Mata
Ringus
Amarsar
Shahpura
Danta Ramgarh
Ralawata
Chaumu
JAIPUR
Narnaul
Rewari
Dharuhera
ARAVALLI RANGES
Katli R.

To Bikaner
To Nagaur
To Ajmer
To Bairat

SHEKHAVATI
RAJASTHAN

RAJASTHAN
INDIA

40 32 24 16 8 0   40   80
KMS.   KMS.

LEGEND:
├─┼─┼─┤   RAILWAY LINES
─────   METALLED ROADS
- - - -   UNMETALLED ROADS
●───●   TOWNS WITH FRESCOES

120 villages of Churu Dist. were
formerly part of Shekhavati

RAJASTHAN is roughly the shape of a diamond, with the great Thar desert at its heart. At the edge of the sand, the rugged Aravalli range turns eastwards, dividing Shekhavati into two unequal parts. Entering Shekhavati diagonally from Danta Ramgarh, the hills stretch to Khandela, Udaipurvati and Khetri, to terminate at Delhi. The presence of this rocky barrier comes as a surprise in this flat and arid landscape, dotted here and there with camel-coloured dunes.

Despite the plain and drab countryside, or perhaps because of it, the desert people fill their lives with colour. Bright reds and yellows flutter across the fields as women sow the seed. Men in saffron, pink and white turbans pursue the plough. Now and then the jagged Aravalli skyline holds a fortress to the eye, a watchtower, an outpost where soldiers once stood alert. For the blood of the Rajputs, the proud members of Rajasthan's warrior clans, was always on the boil: all things were decided on the battlefield. 'Stained with orange turmeric the Rajput rushed into battle maddened with *bhang* [hashish]', the historian Lane Poole tells us.

The mountains with their hideouts were ideal warring country and provided natural bastions. Taking strength from these strategic positions many forts arose, deciding the boundaries within the desert. Although the sixteenth-century Afghan invader Sher Shah Suri is reported to have ruefully remarked after a desert campaign that he had hazarded his empire for a handful of barley, the Rajput looked upon his dry homeland* with pride and sentiment.

All these medieval forts, designed by their builders to be impregnable, were not always so. They often changed hands after dramatic battles. Major segments of the local populace –

* Shekhavati has only one river, which flows during the monsoon. Its name, Katli, comes from the fact that its water 'cuts' through the dry sand.

Camel-drawn ploughs furrow sandy fields near Ratan Nagar as rain clouds gather in the sky. The average annual rainfall in Shekhavati varies from 38 to 45 cm.

The fortified wall of Bhopalgarh Fort on the Aravallis in Khetri. The second wealthiest *Thikana* (feudal state) in Shekhavati, Khetri paid an annual revenue of 80,500 rupees to Jaipur State in 1935.

merchants, jewellers, blacksmiths, cobblers and potters – switched their loyalties to the new rulers and returned to their lifestyles; but the vassals of the Maharaja, the *thakurs**, remained as a nucleus. Maintenance of security under the new regime contined to be their duty.

Douglas Barrett writes:

> This intermittent warfare . . . slowly drained the resources and energy of the smaller courts, but, on the other hand, it produced the Rajput type, proud of his clan, brave and resourceful, and schooled to an inflexible code of honour† which made equal demands on women as on men, for the women in times of desperation were called upon to perform the terrible *jauhar* [group self-immolation] to preserve their chastity unsullied by the enemy. . . . For all his admirable qualities, however, the Rajput had one defect: he could not combine with his fellows against the common enemy.

The Rajput forts now stand conquered by time. The past has slowly turned museum. Stories of battle and bloodshed have become folklore; songs of family pride and valour are sung only by the bards; massive fortified walls guard dwindling treasures. No bugles announce visitors, no flags ride the wind. The clouds in the sky are not from cannon fire.

But in fifteenth-century Rajasthan, horses' hooves sparked on sandstone ramps and valour was blood-red. Swords that now bleed rust in their scabbards were sharp and glinting.

---

* In the old feudal system, most Rajput chieftains held this common title while some possessed other hereditary titles, such as Rao, Raja, Rawal, or Rao Raja. Thakur Nawal Singh of Nawalgarh held the title of 'Bahadur' from the Mughals while Maharaja Man Singh II of Jaipur gave the personal title of 'Rawal' to Thakur Madan Singh of Nawalgarh, Thakur Harnath Singh of Dundlod and Thakur Bagh Singh of Mukundgarh.

† One of the many examples may be cited. In 1679, Sujan Singh, the son of Rao Todarmal who ruled Shekhavati, left his wife on the night of their wedding because the conduct of valour demanded that he go out and defend the Dev Temple at Khandela. And so he fought till death.

The Rajputs

IN SOUTHERN Rajasthan, the declining Chauhan, Parmar and Pratihar dynasties vied with each other for supremacy. In the north, Rana Sanga ruled from Ranthambor to Agra. What was later to be called Shekhavati*, was ruled by a host of military despots and freebooters: Kayamkhanis in Jhunjhunu, Fatehpur, Singhana; Nagar Pathans in Narhar; Nirban Rajputs in Khandela, Poonkh, Udaipurvati, Chhapoli; Chandelas in Rewasa, Kansli; Gaurs in Gaurati. Finally, of these, none remained.

It was the Kachhawahas who were to govern the destiny of Shekhavati. The Kachhawahas, one of the thirty-six major royal houses of India, are *Suryavanshis*, who claim descent from the Sun God. Their most famous ancestor was Rama of Ayodhya, whose life story is recorded in the 24,000 couplets of the epic poem *Ramayana*. The Kachhawahas migrated from Ayodhya to Dausa (near Jaipur) and eventually settled at Amber. In Akbar's reign (1556–1605) they rose in stature, leading the Mughal armies in battle and sharing the rich loot.

A portrait of Rao Shekha-ji (1433–88), who gave Shekhavati its name.

The story of the rise of Shekhavati and of its formation is not without legendary flavour. In the fifteenth century, the ruler of Barwada, a small principality under Amber, was worried about leaving his throne without an heir. This was Mokul Singh, who ruled from 1430 to 1445. In his fifties, disheartened that none of his three wives could bear him a son, he handed over his administration to his officials and became a recluse at Vrindaban, the place sacred to Lord Krishna. There he devoted his time to serving his spiritual master, Madhavswami.

Pleased by his disciple's devotion, the *guru* granted Mokul Singh a wish. In ancient and medieval India this was common practice, for it was believed that learned *gurus* who had achieved communion with God had the power to grant the impossible. Mokul Singh's greatest desire – to have a male heir – now received holy sanction. The *guru* advised him to go home and graze cows in a pasture, as cows were sacred to Lord Krishna. He also presented Mokul with an idol of Gopinath-ji (a manifestation of Krishna as Lord of the Milkmaids) asking him to worship the image by chanting a special *mantra*, or incantation. Accordingly Mokul Singh returned to Barwada and there spent his time grazing cows and worshipping Gopinath-ji, who to this day remains the patron deity of the Shekhavats.

One day Mokul met a Muslim *fakir*, or holy man, called Sheikh Burhan, who was dressed in a blue robe. Sheikh Burhan had come to India in 1398 with Tamerlane†, the plundering Mongol, and had stayed on to propagate Islam among the *Kshatriyas*, or warrior clans. The Sheikh promised a son to Mokul, imposing the strange condition that when the baby boy was born he should be bathed in cow's blood. A son was born in 1433; but with his birth arose a problem: how could Mokul, a devout Hindu, slay a cow to fulfil the Sheikh's whim? To suit his own faith, Mokul Singh substituted for cow's blood that of a goat, in which he bathed the child. Perhaps as compensation, he named his son Shekha, after the Sheikh‡. Mokul also banned the eating of pork, which Hindu religion allows and Muslim religion forbids. He stopped the Hindu practice of *jhatka*, or slaying goats with a single fall of the knife, and adopted the Muslim technique of *halal*, a method of slaying the animal by slow bleeding. In Shekhavati today, the blue flag of the Shekhavats (the colour commemorating that of the *fakir's* robe), the tradition of hanging a

* The Shekhavati area was once a part of Aryavat, the land where the Aryans supposedly composed the Vedas, considered to be the oldest sacred texts in the world. Excavations at Ganasa have recently revealed sites contemporary with Mohen-jo-daro and Harappa dating back to 2000 BC. Inscriptions at Khandela (AD 300), Jeen (AD 692) and Bhuval (AD 865) tell of the continued habitation of this area. In more recent times, just before the formation of Shekhavati, the land north of the Aravallis was called Bagar Pradesh and the land to the south, Dhundhar.

† It was Timur's lame leg that earned him the title 'Timur-i-lang', later distorted by Western historians to Tamerlane.

‡ A century later a similar instance occurred at the Mughal court. Jahangir notes in his memoirs that his father, Akbar, never called him anything but Shekhu Baba, a nickname derived from Sheikh Salim Chisti, who had blessed Akbar with three sons.

calf pendant round the necks of babies, and the name of the place itself, are memories of Sheikh Burhan.

The Sheikh had prophesied that the new-born child would, in time, come to be the ruler of India. But since his condition was not fulfilled, in that goat's blood was used in the bathing, the Sheikh's prophesy could not come true. It is said that the Shekhavats who did rise to prominence were not like the lion – king of the forest – but simply like a billy-goat in a herd of nanny-goats.

The miraculous birth of Shekha led to the equally dramatic founding of Shekhavati (literally the Garden of Shekha). In 1445, when Shekha came to the throne at Barwada, he was twelve years old and ruled over twenty-four villages. Soon after his accession, Shekha met five hundred discontented Panni Pathans, who were passing through his land on their way to Delhi, having left the service of the Muslim rulers of Gujarat. He offered them a group of twelve villages, which came to be called Barah-Basti, and was able to persuade them to settle there. It was this alliance with the Pathans that led to Shekha's meteoric rise. In 1449, he built his fort at Amarsar.

Shekha's family owed token allegiance to the neighbouring state of Amber, from where the famous kings of Jaipur rose. His grandfather, Bala, was the third son of Udaykaran, the thirteenth ruler of Amber, who came to the throne in 1389. When Shekha's father moved away and settled at Barwada, he was given a white mare, on the understanding that its colts would be presented to Amber. It later became customary to send a colt each year, thereby showing acceptance of Amber's superiority. Shekha, once he was sure of his own strength, thought this tradition irksome. He decided to defy it.

Chandra Sen, then ruler of Amber, took Shekha's refusal to send a colt as an open challenge to his power. In 1468 he attacked Barwada with all his forces. Six battles were fought between the cousins, and finally, in 1471, Shekha won. The vanquished army was chased back to Kokus, near Amber. As Shekha gained strength, 'Rao', an honorific prefix, and 'ji', a suffix which is a term of respect, were both added to his name.

Rao Shekha-ji died in 1488 of wounds inflicted while fighting the Gaurs, who had insulted a woman of his clan. By then, his fame had spread beyond Rajasthan and the Shekhavats had become a force to be reckoned with. 'They were accepted as one of the 53 families of the house of the Kachhawahas,' points out Devi Singh Mandawa, a prominent historian of Shekhavati.

Rao Shekha-ji was cremated at Ralawata, adjacent to the tree under which he died, and a *chhatri* was built there. While it was not customary for Hindus to raise memorials for their dead (the Hindus cremate their dead and, in North India, the ashes are scattered in the holy Ganges) a tradition of such cenotaphs *(Plate 44)* and commemorative tablets arose among the Rajput clans. This practice was perhaps inspired by the Muslims, who built imposing tombs for their dead.

Although Rao Shekha-ji's earlier activities had been con-centrated south of the Aravallis, it was Udaipurvati, because of its strategic location, that became the political centre of the Shekhavats. Colonel James Tod, the most prolific historian of Rajasthan, wrote in the early nineteenth century:

> The Shaikhawat confederation, which, springing from the redundant feudality of Amber, through the influence of age and circumstances, has attained a power and consideration almost equalling that of the present State [Jaipur] and although it possesses neither written laws, a permanent congress nor any visible or recognised head, subsists by a sense of common interest. It must not be supposed however, that no system of policy is to be found in this confederation, because the strings are not always visible or in action; the moment any common or individual interest is menaced, the grand council of the barons of Shaikhawati assembles in Udaipur [Udaipurvati] to decide the course of action to be pursued.

In 1562 the Mughal Emperor Akbar had married a princess of Amber (now Jaipur) and harnessed the valiant Rajput forces to his advantage. This alliance had also helped the Amber kings to fill their coffers when they became Commanders-in-Chief of the Mughal army. Even though this policy of Rajput-Mughal amity was later reversed by the religious bigotry of Akbar's great-grandson, Aurangzeb, who in 1679 invaded Marwar, a neighbouring region of Shekhavati, the Amber kings were strong enough to assert themselves. As the Mughal Empire declined after Aurangzeb, shrinking to the size of the principality around Delhi, the Amber kings came to play an increasingly crucial role in the Delhi power struggle. By the time the puppet Mughal monarch Muhammad Shah ascended the throne at Delhi in 1719, Sawai Jai Singh of Amber was very much at the helm of politics.

Having played kingmaker at Delhi, Sawai Jai Singh returned home to enjoy the pleasures of peace. In 1727 he shifted his capital from Amber to found the famous 'pink city' of Jaipur, where art, literature and the Hindu religion flourished under his patronage.

In Shekhavati, nearly three hundred years after Rao Shekha-ji's refusal to pay allegiance to the Amber kings, Maharaja Sawai Jai Singh of Jaipur was able, in 1738, to reassert his suzerainty over the Shekhavats. But his absence was noted. A year later, in 1739, the weakened throne of Delhi was ransacked by Nadir Shah, the Persian plunderer who took with him the famous *Koh-i-Noor* (literally 'Mountain of Light') diamond and the renowned Peacock Throne. An eyewitness remarking on Nadir Shah's looting of Delhi said that 'the accumulated wealth of three hundred and forty-eight years changed masters in a moment'.

Meanwhile, in Rajasthan, the Shekhavats carried on the process of consolidation. Eight generations after Rao Shekha-ji, his descendant Shardul Singh (1681–1742) expanded his territories by ousting the Muslim Kayamkhani nawabs from

Jhunjhunu (1730) and Fatehpur (1731), putting an end to three centuries of Muslim supremacy over large areas of Shekhavati.

The Muslim domination had started in 1384, when the Chauhan Rajputs, who ruled over Dadrera (in the Churu region), were attacked and defeated by Faujdar Sayed Nasir, Nawab of Hissar. The Chauhan ruler, Mota Rao, fled; but his son, Kayam Singh, was captured and brought to Hissar. Nasir converted him to Islam and changed his name to Kayam Khan. After Nasir's death, Kayam Khan became Nawab of Hissar and gained great prestige at the court of the Sultans of Delhi. But his reign was short-lived. Resenting his power, Sultan Kijar Khan had him killed, and his sons, Taj Khan and Mohammed Khan, were chased away from Hissar. They took refuge in Shekhavati, the land of their Rajput ancestors. Mohammed Khan made Jhunjhunu his capital and Taj Khan's son, Fateh Khan, founded

Fatehpur, named after him. The descendants of Kayam Khan became known as the Kayamkhani nawabs.

When Shardul Singh established Hindu Rajput rule over these towns, not only did the Shekhavats extend their own territories, but their renewed alliance with the mighty Jaipur Empire contributed greatly to the strength of both.

In 1775 the Shekhavats allied with the Jaipur army to capture Narnaul and defeat the Mughal army. Yet this alliance once again proved ill-fated. The discontinuation of the law of primogeniture, 125 years before, was by now making itself felt. In 1650, one of the many sons of Todar Mal, the ruler of Udaipurvati, had poisoned his elder brother, Purshotam Das, hoping that he would acquire his property and sit on the throne. But the saddened Todar Mal expelled his murderous son (whose descendants still live in Uttar Pradesh, a northern State of India)

Shardul Singh, the eighth descendant of Rao Shekha-ji, in conference with his five sons. This is a detail from Shardul's cremation *chhatri*, or cenotaph, erected at Parasrampura in 1750, eight years after his death.

Thakur Govind Singh of Chandawal (in Jodhpur State) arriving on elephant-back for his marriage to Baiji Sahiba Sajjan Kumari of Mandawa in 1938. The Nawalgarh Band marches before him. Only one of the many Rolls Royces is visible at the end of the procession. The painted *haveli*, or mansion, is that of Seth Baksh Saraf. It was built in 1906.

and abolished the law of primogeniture, ensuring that future generations would share equally and that brothers would not spill each other's blood.

From then on, land and property were distributed equally among all the sons of the Shekhavats. But, four generations later, this well-intended paternal decree proved shortsighted and in fact rebounded. As diminishing shares were divided among the multiplying progeny, frustration set in. Shekhavati became the seat of personal ambition; freebooters roamed the land, taking whatever came into their hands.

In 1799 an Irish sailor, George Thomas, who had attained prominence at the court of the Nizam of Hyderabad, attacked the Jaipur army at Fatehpur. He established himself at Singhana and nearly succeeded in carving out a kingdom for himself.

The early nineteenth century saw Shekhavati as a lawless land of bandits.

At Jaipur the state of affairs was not much better. From 1818 to 1841, during the long minority of Prince Sawai Jai Singh III, the State of Jaipur was ruled by Rani Bhatiyani, the Prince's mother. According to Harnath Singh Dundlod, a historian of Shekhavati, the Queen, influenced by unscrupulous ministers and slave-girls, let the kingdom run to neglect. The result was that many feudal lords rose against the authority of the State. Local wars flared up. The whole country was ridden with turmoil. Jaipur's army was sent out, but was unable to control the situation*. The British took advantage of the fact that the Treaty of Alliance between the East India Company and Maharaja Jagat Singh of Jaipur had been ratified in 1818† to

send an officer on a special mission to report on the best way to quell the unrest.

The first to tour the area was Lieutenant-Colonel Lockett in 1831. Following his advice, a brigade of British troops was despatched and the administration of Shekhavati taken over. On 17 December 1834, Major P. A. Thoresby was appointed Political Agent in Shekhavati. Lieutenant A. H. E. Boileau reports: 'The Thakurs had then to remit their tribute to the British Treasury: an annual *fauji kharach* [military expense] of half a lakh of rupees [50,000 rupees] was imposed on them for the maintenance of a cavalry contingent. This firm action had an immediate effect and, in 1837, the district was restored to the Jaipur Government.'

The wedding photograph of Kanwar Devi Singh of Mandawa, taken in 1941 before the painted arches of Mandawa Fort. The fort was constructed in 1760, but the frescoes on the exterior were painted in 1800. Kanwar Devi Singh is the seventeenth descendant of Rao Shekha-ji.

An era of relative stability followed, disturbed from time to time by upheavals and subversions. In 1857, during the Mutiny, many Shekhavats sided with the rebels and fought British forces.

Meanwhile at Delhi, as the Mughal Empire crumbled, British ambitions filled the vacuum. The British takeover was not a planned affair. In fact it happened with such subtle transitions that a historian of the period observed, 'conqueror and conquered alike scarcely noted the changes taking place until the patterns of usurpation were irrevocably drawn'.

* Mandawa was attacked in 1823 by the Jaipur forces, but did not fall.

† The Treaty, signed in 1803, provided for a British Resident at Jaipur and amounted to a virtual annexation. However, Jaipur remained a 'Native State' and was never a part of British India. (The term 'native' had no pejorative meaning in the nineteenth century, as it does in India today.)

From the arrival of Sir Thomas Roe, the first English ambassador at the court of Jahangir (1615), to the East India Company's Treaty of Alliance with the Maharaja of Jaipur (1803), there unfolded a takeover with few parallels in history. The British successfully played one power against the other to strengthen their position and rule. The Rajputs' inability to unite and offer joint resistance finally led to their downfall. If it was any compensation, Rajasthan endured longer than the other States, second only to the Punjab.

A fresco of the Manohar Lal Vaid *haveli* (built in 1929 at Chirawa) shows a *seth* with a *tazim*, a flower and an umbrella.

In all these power struggles, the proud Shekhavats may not have emerged as leaders, but neither did they lose their identity. Though they accepted allegiance to the Jaipur State, which bowed first to the Mughals and then to the British, an official publication of the Jaipur Durbar, reviewing its lands as late as 1935, noted: 'the whole State is, so to say, honey-combed with *Thikanas* [feudal states]. But these *Thikana*-lands do not form one solid or continuous mass of territory, rather they are patches spread over the whole length and breadth of the State, surrounded in most cases by state-territory called *Khalsa*, except in Shekhavati Nizamat, almost the whole of which is occupied by Shekhavat *Sirdars*.' It is also significant that in Jaipur State out of ninety-five *Tazimi Sirdars**, who commanded special respect, as many as twenty-two were Shekhavats. Moreover Sikar and Khetri – both in Shekhavati – remained the two richest *Thikanas* of Jaipur.

Kanwar Bhim Singh of Mandawa as a bridegroom, photographed with his gold brocade *achkan* (long coat), *kalgi* (a feathered and jewelled brooch on the turban), the sword and the *tazim*, a hereditary anklet of honour that was normally presented by the Maharaja only to Rajputs. The word *tazim* comes from the Arabic and denotes respect. When a *tazim* holder saluted the Maharaja it was obligatory for the latter to stand and receive the salute. In later years, this honour was also granted to *seths*, or merchants. It was only on rare occasions that two *tazims*, as a mark of double honour, were presented for both ankles.

* This refers to feudal chiefs who wore the hereditary *tazim*, or anklet of honour.

The Marwaris

While the political history of Shekhavati was determined by the warring Rajputs, it would be unfair to consider them the chief architects of their land. The Marwaris, who controlled the funds, remained close at hand.

Literally, the term 'Marwari' means 'inhabitant of Marwar' (in the old Jodhpur State). Because the initial success of the merchants from Marwar, who were the first Rajasthanis to go out and trade, overshadowed that of the merchants from other areas, the term 'Marwari' came to be synonymous with the mercantile class of Rajasthan. This misnomer also applies to the Shekhavati merchants, whose business acumen and success has since far surpassed that of the original merchants from Marwar. The term 'Shekhavat' has come to be applied through usage only to Rajputs.

The relationship between the warriors and the merchants* had mutual advantages: the security offered by the Rajputs drew the Marwaris, and the Marwaris in turn financed the Rajputs to maintain that security. This saved the traders the trouble of maintaining their own armies. There are examples of Hindu Rajput chieftains and Muslim Kayamkhani nawabs vying with each other, pampering the merchant community, and pleading with it to settle on their territory†. Thomas A. Timberg, in his recent research on the Marwaris, writes, 'in their home fiefs of Shekhavati, merchants were granted gold anklets and substantive privileges in the way of exemption from customs, search and seizure, and even criminal processes. They were granted state convoys for their goods and charters for charitable enterprises like schools.' This relationship of mutual benefit worked for many years. Through Shekhavati, caravans and trading convoys moved freely between the Gujarat coast and Delhi and, on the southern Silk Route, between the Middle East and China. Apart from the safe passage provided by the Rajputs to the merchants, the common traveller often availed himself of the security offered by the convoys of the *charans* and *bhats* (bards and genealogists), whose sacred character is said to have overawed the lawless of the wild and desolate regions. Many years of brisk commerce brought more than just prosperity. Security, and a favourable geographical position, helped the towns of Shekhavati to play the part of the fourteenth- and fifteenth-century Hanse towns of Europe. A traveller of the past observed:

> The productions of India, Cashmere, and China, were interchanged for those of Europe, Africa, Persia and Arabia. Caravans from the ports of Cutch and Guzerat imported elephants' teeth, copper, dates, gum-arabic, borax, coco-nuts, broadcloths, silks, sandalwood, camphor, dyes, drugs, oxide and sulphuret of arsenic, spices, coffee, etc. In exchange they exported chintzes, dried fruit, *jeeroh* [cumin], asafoetida from Mooltan, sugar, opium, silks and fine cloth, potash, shawls, dyed blankets, arms and salt of home manufacture.

G. D. Birla, the patriarch of the richest family-held empire in India, as a young man. The Birla family had its beginnings in Pilani.

The Shekhavati Marwaris were known to trade in quantity at very low percentages, but obviously their profits were large enough for them to turn into prolific builders: the abundance of public wells and reservoirs, cowsheds, schools, temples and caravanserais they commissioned in their home towns was proof of their philanthropic instinct. For themselves, they built opulent *havelis*, or mansions, and sometimes whimsical little gardens – a considerable luxury in an area where a pail of water had to be

* Traditional Indian society is divided into four broad castes: *Brahmins*, or priests; *Kshatriyas*, or warriors (this includes the Rajputs); *Vaishyas*, or merchants (this includes the Marwaris); and the *Sudras*, or manual labourers.

† As a rule, the forts were built earlier than the *havelis*, signifying that security preceded active trade: Amarsar (1449), Fatehpur (1521), Manoharpura (1577), Sikar (1687), Nawalgarh (1731), Bissau (1746), Sultana (1747), Dundlod (1750), Khetri and Gyangiasar (1755), Mandawa (1760), Malsisar (1762), Mahansar (1768), Surajgarh (1799). Though the Mughals did not allow four fortified walls to be erected round the forts of their vassals, Singhana, Narhar, Jhunjhunu and Fatehpur took advantage of the weakness of the later Mughals to build the fourth wall.

drawn from a hundred metres below the ground to keep alive the few struggling plants.

Had the purpose of their enormous *havelis* been simply for use as domiciles, much less elaborate structures would have sufficed. But, besides being a visible extravagance, the *havelis* were an obvious, albeit affectionate, gesture by the travelling tradesmen to compensate their families. At the same time it ensured the rigid seclusion of women and encouraged thrift – both crucial features of Marwari success. In later years, observes Timberg, once wealth was accumulated in Shekhavati, there was 'a shift towards the larger towns, reflecting the imperatives of consumption rather than of accumulation.'

Seth Vijay Narayan Biyani of Sikar seated before his *haveli*. His *dhoti, kurta* and turban are the typical dress of the business community of Shekhavati. Sikar was the wealthiest *thikana* of Shekhavati. Its annual gross income in 1935 amounted to 1,187,709 rupees.

Traditionally, the Marwaris financed and serviced the princely courts, conducted entrepot trade in Rajasthan and expanded their business beyond. By 1860 British power was firmly entrenched all over India, affecting Marwaris on all three fronts: the British overshadowed the princely courts; British customs barriers cut off entrepot markets; British goods outmoded Indian goods. Rajasthan, once a rich land for traders, became a commercial desert.

The Opium War in China (1839–42) had blocked the Indian outlet for this intoxicant. Trade in indigo was declining now that synthetic blue dye had begun to arrive from Germany. For the local merchant there remained only petty trade, with little security. Apart from this, overland trade routes were being replaced by river and rail routes. If the traders stayed back, they would stagnate. With their keen sense of business, merchants and traders began to move out, mainly to the ports.

For a community naturally schooled in the ethic of commerce, obstacles were turned into opportunities. Marwari migration, beginning as a trickle, soon became a virtual exodus. The early movement was eastwards, to Bihar, Assam and the Central Provinces – areas where jute, cotton and wool were potentially in exportable surplus. To places where opportunities proved scarce, or competition stiff, as in Bombay, the Marwaris moved less rapidly.

While the Rajputs rose by fighting others of their clan, the Marwaris possessed the admirable but rare trait of promoting others of their community. When the young men first left their desert villages in Rajasthan they were frequently cared for by other Marwaris. The rise of the Birla family in Pilani, which today controls the single biggest family-held industrial empire in India, was prompted by Marwari compatriots. In Calcutta, Shiv Narain Birla, grandfather of the present family patriarch G. D. Birla, first stayed in a *basa* (charitable kitchen) run by the Sarafs of Mandawa and the Jhunjhunwalas of Chirawa, leading cloth merchants of the time.

By the 1870s Marwari prosperity was an acknowledged fact. From their early days as small-town shopkeepers, the Marwaris carried their values of financial conservatism and social orthodoxy into an international arena of trade and investment.

Unlike the history of the Rajputs, the story of every other Marwari family is one of co-operation and success. A history of the Marwaris would essentially be elaborate family chronicles, each one a book in itself.

The people

While wars and treaties decided the fate of a few and the allegiance of many, the condition of the peasantry remained unchanged. The armies trampled their fields and plundered their grain on their way to beseige forts and loot towns. The farmers sowed their millet and lived modestly. Holi, Gangor, Teej and

Dussehra*, the local festivals, brought a change, and occasional fairs relieved the monotony. But in general the life of the peasant simply moved with the seasons.

Summer was harsh and hostile. The vast desert lived up to its Sanskrit name, *Marusthal* – region of death. The wells were almost dry, the water often sinking to a depth of a hundred metres. Long lines of willing hands were used to draw a single pail. Oxen and camels were employed to irrigate the dry, cracked furrows. A little rain fell, a peasant lamented in a folk song: 'this rain has wet only one horn of my cow, not the other'. The heat banished the people indoors. With tightly shut houses and desolate streets, the entire area bore the appearance of a ghost settlement.

In southern Rajasthan rain gods are commonly invoked in the fields, cow dung smeared on their sacred faces. Legend has it that the gods must wash the dung off their own faces by making it rain. But the gods were not always concerned: the dung caked and peeled on their cheeks; the earth baked the seeds in the soil. Dreams of the harvest were stillborn. This was the *jal kaal*, or drought, not uncommon in Rajasthan. Hunger could not be postponed, so, as the weeks passed, a slow exodus began. Lean, sunburnt peasants trickled across the 'region of death', their cows and goats emaciated to the bones.

When thirst and famine forced farmers to migrate *en masse* from villages, towns became saturated with people hunting for jobs. The cities became cruel and heartless. Unlived, the season passed until the farmers returned home, drawn by the voice of their ancestral lands. They could not bring themselves to abandon the soil of their birth, for who would bear the consequences of this unholy deed?

But, when the rains came, the rain gods were forgotten. The clouds moved like spirits darkening the skies at noon. Peacocks appeared like birds of fantasy and shook their fanned tails into a dance. The monsoon filtered the air. In years of good rain, the *johras*, or reservoirs, were full to overflowing. The swings in the green trees rang with the laughter of children.

It was not only the conscience of the farmer that did not allow him to leave his ancestral land. It was also a conservatism born of years of poverty and suffering. While the farmer remained caught in this vicious web, the merchant was able to walk out, and, by his shrewd and timely moves, improve his fate. Thus farmers continued to live in mud huts with thatched roofs as Marwaris built enormous *pukka havelis* that even by today's standards seem gigantic and almost surreal in a barren desert landscape.

* The four major festivals of Shekhavati are:

Holi Originally associated with the demoness Holika who is ritually burnt on the eve of the festival of colours, Holi has also come to be popularly associated with Krishna and the *gopis*. The throwing of coloured powder and liquids through water pistols is believed to be a vestige of an ancient fertility rite.
Gangor The spring festival of Gangor is held in honour of Gauri, an aspect of Parvati. She and her consort Isar-ji are dressed and carried in procession.
Teej A women's festival held in honour of Parvati (Shiva's wife), Teej also celebrates the beginning of the monsoon. Women dressed in red play with the children on swings hung from the trees.
Dussehra This festival symbolizes the triumph of Rama over the demon-king Ravana. Each of the first nine nights of the festival is dedicated to a different aspect of the goddess Durga, whose help Rama sought in his battle. On the tenth night, effigies of Ravana and his two brothers are stuffed with firecrackers and burnt.

The *havelis*

THE WORD *haveli*, which is of Persian origin, means 'a surrounded or an enclosed place'. It has no exact equivalent in the English language. Perhaps 'mansion' comes close enough, suggesting the spacious residence that a *haveli* connotes, but it fails to capture the essence of a way of life that was more than just a form of architecture. In Mughal times it signified a residential block, usually three to five storeys high, around an open courtyard. It normally accommodated several families who lived together as an economic, civic and social unit, sharing many common amenities. The density of occupation was balanced by the open court that would usually accommodate a common well for drinking-water, space for washing and drying clothes, and a play area for children. Just as the joint family system was the smallest economic unit in the social structure of medieval India, a *haveli** was the smallest survival unit in the civic structure.

Havelis are generally town houses, as opposed to *kothis*, or garden houses of the suburbs. The original function of a *haveli*,

* *Haveli* was also the name given to the temples of Rajasthan's Vallabhachari sect which are incorporated in the home of the chief priest. Such temples are normally private to members of the sect. It was probably their 'walled-in' aspect and their use as residences that combined to lend them the name of *haveli*. (Robert Skelton)

An aerial view of a *char chowk haveli*, a mansion with four courtyards, built in the early nineteenth century by Ram Lal Murlidhar Ganeriwala in Lachhmangarh. This *haveli*, which looks austere and unfriendly from the outside, served as a fortified home, though it was not necessarily armed. It was designed to have an inward aspect: small windows looked out into the street and larger ones opened on to the courtyards. Some rooms on the first floor were made without roofs so that the summer nights could be spent in privacy under the starry sky. The plan of Lachhmangarh, with its parallel streets and large squares at the crossroads, was modelled on that of Jaipur.

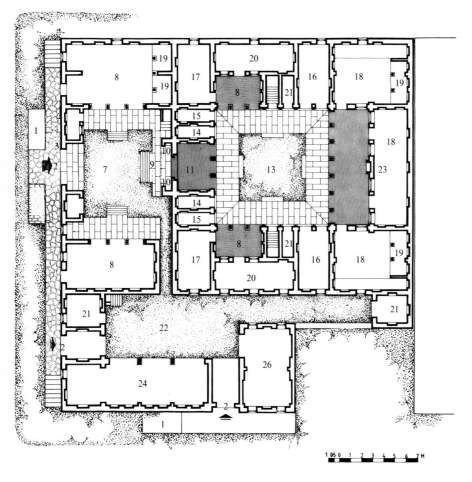

Floor plan of the Sagarmal Gulab Rai Ladia *haveli*

1. khurra (ramp)
2. darujo (doorway)
3. kulli (stone pillar supporting the gate hinges)
4. mori (small door within a large gate)
5. jalalia (gate stopper)
6. todi (stone bracket)
7. chowk (courtyard – outer)
8. tibari (a three-arched verandah) or baithak (when doors have been inserted)
9. deodhi (entrance to the ladies' appartments)
10. gokha (place for sitting outside the entrance)
11. poli (entrance hall)
12. rahose (inner balcony)
13. chowk (courtyard – inner)
14. parinda (water room)
15. hamam (bath room)
16. rasoi or rasora (kitchen)
17. sal (room inside a tibari without windows)
18. chogra (bedroom)
19. duchhatti (loft)
20. bakhari (space for storage)
21. kotri (store room)
22. nora (cattle-pen)
23. pitar-ji ko mandh (temple of one's ancestors)
24. than (covered cattle-shed)
25. chandni (roofless room)
26. dhara (haystock)
27. chhat (terrace)
28. dagli (small room on the terrace covering the stairs)
29. jharokha (overhanging balcony)
30. ghubaria (space below ground level for rubbish)

apart from providing a residence, was to wall in the domestic life of a family. Secluded from the outside world, a *haveli* set its own pace of life. All through royal and feudal India the *havelis*, whether inhabited by Hindus or Muslims, represented the rigid lifestyle of a society that segregated its men from its women. The architecture of the *haveli* was conceived around this social norm. Unlike the Mughal *havelis*, the typical *haveli* in Shekhavati consists of two courtyards – an outer and an inner. The grander ones sometimes had three or four courtyards.

Today, life in the *haveli* continues on much the same pattern, though there are fewer inhabitants. The outer courtyard serves as an extended threshold, since the main gate is seldom shut. The inner one is the domain of the women, who are entirely occupied with household chores. In days gone by, their routine began before dawn with the worship of *tulsi*, or holy basil, followed by the milking of the cows in the *nora*, or pen, the churning of butter, cooking, collecting and storing water in a special airy room called the *parinda*. When male guests entered the house, the women, who normally remained in *purdah* (literally, 'behind the curtain'), retreated briskly into the *zenana*, their private

apartments. And from their fretted *zenana* windows they peeped into the men's world. This forced seclusion of women was apparently introduced after the Muslim invasions.

Just as the *purdah* covered their faces from the male members of the family, the inner courtyard hid them from the world. Rama Mehta, in her book *Inside the Haveli*, tells us that 'young maids were not allowed outside the courtyard until they were married . . . all the women, young and old, had their faces covered even when no men were in sight. The only women who moved around freely with faces uncovered were the daughters of the family.' Their home was their world, their boundary; they seldom went out, even to attend a wedding. Servants normally did the daily shopping, or vendors brought their wares to the door. The keys to the provisions remained with the oldest woman, who also supervised the kitchen. In the Rajput *havelis*, *badarans*, or trusted maidservants, took care of the house (and this became a hereditary position), while the ladies of the house tended the children. In the Marwari *havelis*, it was not uncommon for *newagans*, or washerwomen, to look after the children and give the ladies a gentle oil massage.

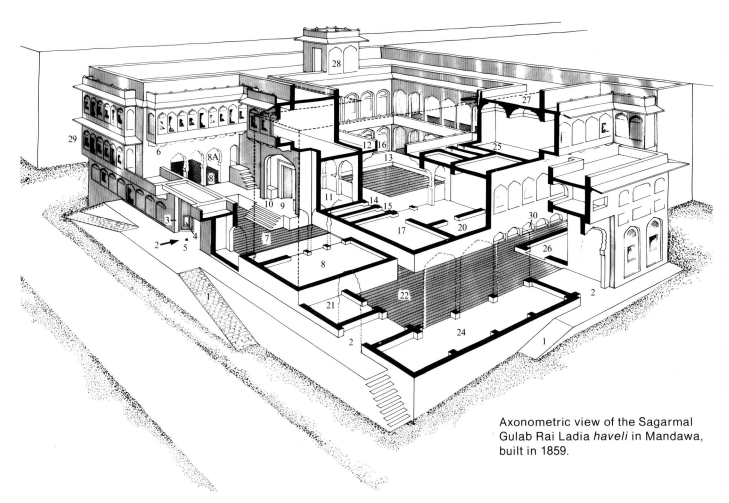

Axonometric view of the Sagarmal
Gulab Rai Ladia *haveli* in Mandawa,
built in 1859.

The men of the *haveli* disappeared at dawn. All day they worked in town, or held office in a special section of the *haveli* called the *tibari* or *baithak (see page 23)*. At meal-times they returned to the interior. But even when they were away, their presence was felt throughout the *haveli*. Nothing was done without their consent, and it was around their desires that the whole routine of the house revolved.

Visitors removed their shoes on entering the *haveli* and sat cross-legged on the mattresses. Even today it is a tradition for the inhabitants of a *haveli* to remain barefoot.

The rooms of the *haveli* are not always linked to one another. Doors lead out to the courtyard, or, on the first floor, to a fenced overhanging balcony that runs above the courtyard on all four sides. Two or more flights of steps, depending on the size of the *haveli*, lead to the terrace. Sometimes, first-floor rooms were built roofless, to let in the pleasant desert night while preserving privacy.

To meet the social and climatic needs, a system of windows at three levels was evolved. The lowest windows provided a view outside. Often louvred or fretted, they enabled the women to look out unobserved. The second level of windows was higher, to let in the light without the glare, often through coloured glass. The third, the highest, was also the smallest; its carved grilles helped the air to circulate: as the air in the room got warmer, it rose to let a fresh breeze move in through the doors and lower windows. This movement of air made the indoor conditions more pleasant.

Besides being functional, the *havelis* had their own decor and ornamentation. Main doors and brackets were intricately carved; frescoes covered every surface: the façade, gateways, courtyard walls, parapets and ceilings. Sometimes an inner room carried delicately gilded paintings. Occasionally, in the sleeping apartments – the only place where husband and wife came into uninhibited contact – erotic paintings were commissioned. These were meant to be admired behind locked doors. Otherwise, there was little to fill the room. The concept of furniture did not exist. Usually there were open, arcaded *tibaris* on one or both sides of the entrance. Here the men sat and conducted business from the house. The rooms were almost bare and, like other parts of the *haveli*, were usually furnished with

The façade of the Sed Mal Sarawgi *haveli* in Nawalgarh shows the painted entrance with three symmetrical arches and windows on each side. The tableaux between the brackets depict mythological scenes; under the parapets are portraits of prominent men and women.

large cotton mattresses placed on the floor and covered with white sheets. Bulky white bolsters served as back-rests. These sparsely furnished rooms lent themselves to a profusion of ornamentation.

The chaplain of the first embassy which England sent to India, three and a half centuries ago, wrote of the lack of furniture: 'For they have no chairs, stools, couches, tables, beds enclosed with canopies, or curtains, in any of their rooms. And the truth is, that if they had them, the extreme heat would forbid the use of many of them.' The chaplain's remark proved to be less true once the British influence spread in Rajasthan. *Havelis*, after the turn of the century, began to be furnished with copies of heavy European furniture, ornate mirror frames, chandeliers, anglicized glass paintings, lithographs and 'imported' lace curtains.

The inhabitants of the *haveli* developed a great tradition of refined hospitality. *Atithi satkar* (honouring the visitor) meant undivided attention for a guest who had crossed into the *deohri*,

or threshold, of a *haveli*. He was greeted with sherbet and sweetmeats and given the best room with the most comfortable bed. All the tastiest delicacies of the *haveli* were offered, and the meal ended with special *paans* (betel leaf with lime, pieces of areca nut, tobacco and other ingredients). These were presented in silver *paandans* (intricately worked boxes), which kept the *paans* fresh. Hospitality did not end here. Later, in the guest's room, on the terrace or in the courtyard in summer, the finest *hookahs* were prepared. Silver, brass and wooden bases were attached to earthen *chillums* and the opium and tobacco smoked through pipes adorned with golden threads.

Music was played far into the night. While the orthodox Marwaris stopped at food and music, the Rajputs often invited court dancers and *ghazal* singers and entertained with liquor. In the absence of public places for entertainment it was quite normal to invite women artistes to the *haveli*; there was no connotation of vice in such entertainment.

The techniques

The mural culture in India dates back many centuries. Several of the earliest examples, from the second century BC onwards, survive at Ajanta, Bagh, Badami and elsewhere. *(For the sites and chronology of wall paintings in India, see page 113).* The techniques varied from one area to another, depending primarily on the raw materials available.

The technique employed for the Shekhavati frescoes was elaborate, by any standard, and similar to the Italian fresco technique developed around the fourteenth century. According to R. A. Agarawala, author of *Marwar Murals*, in the Italian method water was used with the pigments so that, through a chemical process, the lime surface acted as an adhesive. In the Rajasthani method the colours were mixed in lime water or lime plaster and were then made to sink into the plaster through a manual process of beating, burnishing and polishing. Whether the art travelled to North India through the Mughals, who knew of it from Persia, or whether foreign missionaries to the Mughal court first introduced it at Fatehpur Sikri, is not known. It is also possible that the technique came from South India, where the art of *fresco buono*, or painting on wet plaster, was known during the Chola and Nayak dynasties (eleventh to seventeenth centuries). However, the local Shekhavati mason had definitely mastered it to produce the authentic *fresco buono*, and the results were spectacular and rewarding: the fresco became almost as durable as the building it adorned.

In Shekhavati the fresco painters are called *chiteras*, and belong to the caste of *Kumhars*, or potters. They are also called *chejaras*, or masons, since they performed both the functions of painting and building. When they undertook to paint a *haveli* or a temple they normally worked in groups of three or four under the supervision of a master, a tradition not unlike the royal ateliers where miniatures were painted. The earliest frescoes, as at the garden lodge at Bairat in Alwar District (around 1610), the Parasrampura cenotaph (1750), the interiors of Mandawa Fort (around 1760), or the well *chhatris* in Chirawa (around 1820), used natural pigments: *kajal* (lamp black) for black; *safeda* (chalk) or *chuna* (lime) for white; *neel* (indigo) for blue; *harabhata (terra verte)* for green; *geru* (a red stone powder) for red; *hirmich* (an earthy mineral) for brown; *kesar* (saffron) for orange; and *pevri* (yellow clay) for yellow ochre. This last colour was also obtained by the unique method of evaporating the collected urine of cows fed for ten days on mango leaves. The resulting paste was made into balls called *gau golis*, which gave a very brilliant yellow when diluted with water. This preparation was later banned as the process proved damaging to the health of cows, considered holy by the Hindus.

All these colours, normally preserved in a dry form, were, when required, mixed into a paste and applied to the already wet surface of the wall. In the technique of the *fresco buono*, or true fresco, this was much less tedious than the preparation of the wall itself. To ensure that the joins did not show, the artist and the mason had to co-ordinate their work to complete a picture at a single stretch.

In the *fresco buono* method, known in Rajasthan as *ala gila* or *arayish*, the mortar for the walls of brick or stone was prepared from a very fine clay. This was usually gathered from ant hills or prepared by sifting clay through a fine gauze. A layer of this mixture, about a centimetre thick, was first plastered on the wall and allowed to dry, before a second layer was applied. For the third coat of mortar, finely cut pieces of hessian were added to the

Two men work simultaneously on restoring and repainting the wall of a *haveli*. The mason below applies a fresh coat of lime while the artist proceeds with the painting.

mixture and smoothed on to the wall with a trowel. Before the surface dried, it was incised at intervals so that the many layers of plaster that were to follow could adhere to the mortar.

The first layer of plaster would consist of one-fourth of *kali*, lime from Ranoli, carried to Shekhavati from an area near Jaipur, and three-fourths of gravel or of brick dust. This was applied to the wall after it had been thoroughly drenched. The next coat consisted of one-fourth of lime mixed with three-fourths of marble dust from Makrana, the renowned mines which supplied the pure white marble for the Taj Mahal. This was followed by a drying period which set the plaster.

The final layer, again applied to a wet wall, consisted of fine lime dust, filtered and refiltered, and made into a paste by adding *chhachh* (sour buttermilk) and *gur* (jaggery). Between each plastering, the surface was burnished with agate or a white stone, which, in Shekhavati, came from Bhasawa in Sikar district.

While the top layer was still damp, the design was drawn and painted. As the wall dried, a chemical reaction occurred between plaster and pigment, sealing the painting with the plaster, so that they became one. The effectiveness of this technique is demonstrated by the survival of a great many frescoes after two or three hundred years of exposure. Since it was essential that the plaster be wet, only a limited amount of the final layer – enough to take a day's painting – was applied at one time. A close examination of some frescoes reveals the joins, where one day's work ended and the next began. If the artist made a mistake, changed his mind about a detail or simply did less work than he had intended, the dried top layer had to be peeled away and replaced with fresh, damp plaster.

To avoid *pentimenti*, which sometimes peep through thin layers of paint, a method of tracing was devised. Drawings on paper were pin-pricked along the outlines of the design, in order to create a stencil, called *khaka*. This was placed against the wall and rubbed with charcoal or brick dust to produce a dotted line. Which served as a base for the black outlines; the colours were put in later. (Michelangelo's method was different: he held the paper drawing against the wall and pressed over the lines with a stylus, making faint grooves.) Before the paint dried, it was pounded with a piece of wood so that the paint would penetrate into the surface.

The final touches came after the drying: a quick rubbing of agate fixed the colour, followed by a coat of coconut oil, or simply of crushed coconut, applied with a soft cloth. The fresco was thus covered and preserved with a transparent veneer that dulled but did not disappear with sun and rain.

Given the speed with which the artists had to work, the fresco was bound to be an art of broad effects rather than of exquisite detail. And yet the Shekhavati artists could display immense skill when specially commissioned to paint intricate frescoes in a private room of a *haveli* or a fort, in the inner shrine of a temple or on the ceiling of a grand cenotaph.

In later years, around 1890, when synthetic dyes from Germany and England appeared, the technique of the *fresco buono* had to be abandoned, since the artificial pigments reacted adversely with the damp walls. It was replaced by the *fresco-secco*, or tempera, technique of painting on dry plaster. The local artists were already familiar with this technique as they had earlier used the method of dry fresco in the interior of rooms and on walls which were adequately protected from the sun and rain.

Gradually, even this simpler *fresco-secco* process died out with the patrons' change of heart. The acceleration of modernization in India brought with it the final breakdown of traditional relationship between patron and artist. *Pax Britannica* never took over the role of the sensitive 'royal' patron and indeed it could not, for an essential feature of the patron-artist relationship had always been a mutual sharing of well-known cultural symbols and aesthetic values. With the turn of the century, the patronage gradually weakened and faded. The printing press brought by the British, together with photography, sounded the death knell of traditional painting. Even the rural Indian could now purchase cheap reproductions and oleographs, especially of popular Hindu gods and goddesses. Traditional painters were forced to move to other professions.

The background

In the beginning, the desert offered only its blank palette. There is no record of a distinct school of painting in Shekhavati before the frescoes. History took up this colourless page and, through a series of interactions, made Shekhavati blossom with frescoes. But then, after a short span of some two hundred years, the art was lost and history passed by – a silent, unparticipating spectator.

The Shekhavati frescoes were influenced by the Jaipur and

An artist mixes and prepares his colours in earthen pots.

Mughal schools of painting, which in turn had been inspired by Persian art. A study of the art styles and forms of the desert States and the royal Mughal court at Delhi and Agra reveals a series of exchanges. The initiation of the Mughal studio in Delhi probably took place in the reign of Humayun, after he returned from the Safavid court in Persia, bringing with him Persian master painters, illuminators and bookbinders. Under his successor, Akbar, Hindu painters were recruited from all over India, mingling the many traditions in the royal ateliers. As the strength and influence of the Mughal court grew, more leading craftsmen brought Indian architectural traditions into Mughal building practices and in particular Rajput styles into Mughal painting.

Akbar's marriage in 1562 to Harka Bai of Jaipur brought Rajput blood into the dynasty itself, to forge an even stronger link. Akbar's Fatehpur Sikri, a far cry from the Muslim concepts of order and symmetry, is a fine example of the coming together of the two styles. Flouting the Muslim tradition which precludes the depiction of life (as outlined in the *Hadith*, a compilation of the sayings of the Prophet), Jodha Bai's private apartments at Fatehpur Sikri were apparently painted with frescoes containing figures, of which little remains now. Also, Akbar's hunting lodge *(Plate 65)* at Bairat, in Alwar District, is ornately painted with human figures, birds, animals and even Hindu deities and mythological representations. It was Akbar who understood better than anyone else that if the interaction were to work it would have to be generously reciprocal. If he were to harness the skills of his Hindu subjects (which formed the majority), he could not forbid the spontaneous outflow of their imagery and reference symbols. (Only a liberal, enlightened Muslim monarch could have commissioned the *Ramayana* and *Mahabharata* in Persian.) In his far-sighted recognition of this fact lay the magnetism which drew anyone of significance to his court.

Shah Jahan, the next great Mughal builder, continued the Rajasthani bias: both his mother and his grandmother had been Rajput princesses. When Aurangzeb reversed the established religous tolerance of the Mughals, his move had far-reaching effects in the field of art. It can be argued that this was not, in fact, what Aurangzeb had intended. The letter which he dictated from his death-bed is full of repentance. He had contrived to become sovereign by murder, and by having his brothers arrested. To alleviate these crimes perhaps he felt compelled to take refuge in orthodox religion, threatening Hindu conversions by the sword. Labour left the fields, the looms of industry were abandoned and the doors of the royal ateliers were bolted. The artists surged out, to colour the palettes of the neighbouring courts. The traditions which had once contributed to Akbar's ateliers now returned enriched with Mughal-Persian influences.

Later, Sawai Jai Singh's newly founded city of Jaipur welcomed the few artists, craftsmen, poets, writers, musicians and law givers who had remained in the hope of seeing better days at Delhi but were now fleeing the weakened Mughal court

An architect's sketch of the façade of a building, showing in the foreground the frescoes. Frescoes were first drawn on paper, the lines were then perforated with a pin to form a stencil, which was placed on the wall and rubbed with charcoal. This produced a dotted tracing on the wall that served as an outline for the artist.

of Mohammad Shah. Although Shekhavati had by this time been enveloped once more into the folds of Jaipur, it was nevertheless away from the luxuries and patronage of the court. Years of comparative peace, prosperity and security in Shekhavati gave birth to its own patrons – the traders who built elaborate painted *havelis* with the enormous wealth they had accumulated along the trade routes and at the ports. The frescoes sprang up through a patronage peculiar to itself: much money had been generated by these desert people, and for sentimental reasons they wished to spend it on their home towns. This naturally also brought them social prestige.

While most other schools of painting in Rajasthan have restricted themselves to miniatures on paper, ivory and wood (with the exception of some frescoes on palaces and temples), the Shekhavati paintings are on quite another scale. Here the miniature paintings grow from the diminutive, almost as if they had flown into the streets and stretched themselves to life size. Royal elephants bedecked in regalia, splendid horses and camels parade with superbly attired persons in a pageantry that records an era now left behind.

The wall paintings of Shekhavati are not seasonal or ritualistic, though for the layman they seem as decorative as the paintings of Madhubani in Bihar, Warli in Maharashtra, Chhota Udaipur in Gujarat, and others. On the popular, impermanent wall paintings, Pupul Jayakar comments:

> The adornment of the walls of the home by use of earth plaster, mirrors, seeds, reliefs in clay, the painting of the walls with icons of the Puranic gods and with ornamental forms of birds, serpents, flowers and geometric diagrams exist in areas where the clay walls of village huts provide a canvas for such decoration . . . the walls of the hut, the street, the shop and the market place become the picture gallery, the canvas on which the records of the race, the exploits of god and hero are maintained. But the paintings are transitory and anonymous. They appear on the walls, fade, are whitewashed over and reappear with the cyclic movement of the seasons and the related rituals.

In contrast to these seasonal paintings for rituals and ceremonies the frescoes of Shekhavati are as permanent as the walls they adorn. The earliest ones in Shekhavati are found in the forts which are the oldest standing structures of the area. Among these the forts of Sikar, Nawalgarh, Dundlod, Mandawa (*Plate 69*), Malsisar, Khetri, Surajgarh (*Plate 57*) and Shahpura still have early examples of frescoes. Despite the fact that the Rajputs spent more time in battle than in patronizing the arts, one of the first and most outstanding frescoes in Shekhavati, dated 1750, is found on a Rajput cenotaph – that of Shardul Singh at Parasrampura (*Plates 24, 25, 26, 42*). Other cenotaphs with painted *chhatris* appear in most towns, but those built to commemorate the Marwari merchants of Bissau and Ramgarh (*Plates 44, 45*) are prominent. Another kind of *chhatri*, not in its mortuary form, appears as a little canopied kiosk that provided shelter by a well. Of these the two finest examples of painted ceilings are to be found in Chirawa (*Plates 47, 48*) while Malsisar (*Plate 50*) has a different example of a closed *chhatri* painted on the outside.

The typical Shekhavati wells (*Plate 46*) announce the presence of water with four tall minarets, often painted in bold black lines and sometimes including a simple portrait of Hanuman. A long slope, equivalent to the depth of the well in the driest season, enables the villagers to draw water by pulling ropes or by using camels and bullocks on the gradients. Since the water level is normally low the interiors of the wells are also occasionally painted. Perhaps the best examples of these are the Harlalka and Aggarwal wells of Mandawa. Sometimes, faded frescoes remain on the *johras* built to gather rainwater. The

paintings on the Ojha *johra* in Baggar (*Plate 49*) still hold out against the elements.

Frescoes are also commonly found in temples that exist in almost all the towns of Shekhavati. Of these, early examples appear in Khetri (*Plates 51, 64*), Ramgarh (*Plate 54*), Malsisar (*Plates 53, 55, 67*), Gyangyasar and Chirawa. Those at Dundlod have now been covered with whitewash.

Not every *haveli* is painted; in particular, many of the later ones in Mandrela, Churi Ajitgarh, Chirana and Kanjara stand lime-white and graphic against the changing skies of Shekhavati.

Perhaps the single most outstanding example of a painted *haveli* is the *Soné Chandi ki haveli* (painted in 1846), which belongs to the Podars of Mahansar (*frontispiece and Plate 52*). Its foremost room, a 'T' shaped hall which is reputed to have been the showroom of a jeweller, gives it its name, which means 'the house of gold and silver'. Gilded strappings and mirrored ceilings create a bewildering opulence around finely painted frescoes, which are mainly of mythological subjects. Exquisite floral friezes border the lower half of the wall, and an intricately carved central wooden beam supports the ceiling. An equally fine fresco, possibly by the same hand, is painted on the ceiling of a dome in the old fort of Nawalgarh which depicts an aerial view of the city of Jaipur.

The themes

A study of the thematic content of the Shekhavati frescoes, from the earliest examples at Parasrampura (1750) to the later ones of the British period (1930), reveals the changing tastes of the painters and their patrons.

In all likelihood, the painter had a free hand, because the purpose of the fresco was not ideological or biographical, but decorative. The fact that Muslim subjects were painted on Marwari *havelis* makes it evident that the patrons were quite tolerant, and that they respected the artist's choice of subject. This could include common themes such as guards in Mughal attire (*Plate 5a*), *mahouts* (elephant drivers) and *nawabs* (Muslim princelings) and the more Islamic subjects like the *Barraq*, the mare with a lady's face, which was the vehicle by which Mohammed ascended to Heaven. This secularism was, however, not reciprocated on the Muslim *havelis*, though their frescoes unconsciously borrowed Hindu motifs. An exception to the decorative frescoes is the biographical example painted inside the dome of the Parasrampura *chhatri* (*Plate 24*). Here Shardul Singh's life is depicted, not chronologically, but through a juxtaposition of anecdotes, the emphasis being on the martial aspect. This is understandable for several reasons: the *chhatri* was built by Shardul Singh's wife as a commemorative monument; it was built at a time when his fame was at its height and people recalled and narrated his conquests. Shardul Singh's role as a Hindu Rajput was of great significance in the wake of the

Hindu-Muslim rivalry that had been reignited by the Mughal emperor Aurangzeb. Shardul's humbling of the Muslim Kayamkhanis and the Nagar Pathans was an important turning-point. Also, the procession of Shardul's army was a subject that ideally lent itself to a grand circular treatment for the interior of a dome.

Since the period in which the frescoes flourished (1830–1900) was longer than that of their decline and discontinuation (1900–30), the forts, *havelis*, *chhatris* and temples are dominated by the earlier frescoes. Generally speaking, this was the era of mythological frescoes interspersed with illustrations of local legends, animals, portraits, hunting and wrestling scenes, and glimpses of everyday life.

Within these broad outlines, the subjects were picked at random. Gods and heroes from completely different texts regularly appear in adjoining tableaux. Usually, the artist's choice was determined not so much by the subject matter as by the treatment it could take. For example, the most popular folk tale of the love of Dhola and Maru lends itself to a linear treatment, because the lovers are chased by the army of Oomar Soomra *(Plate 75)*. Similarly, a train can conveniently fill a horizontal panel. So Dhola-Maru and a train, incongruous as this may be, can appear together, with scrolling foliage, floral patterns and a few mythological panels thrown in.

Few *havelis* carried only floral and geometrical designs. This could have been the patron's preference, as in the case of the Mangal Chand Dalmia *haveli* in Chirawa *(Plate 37)*, or it could have been unavoidable, as in the Mamli Khan *mahal* in Baggar. Mamli Khan was a Muslim nawab and was therefore bound by Islamic tradition to use no figurative decoration for his frescoes.

The blank spaces between the doors, windows, brackets and other architectural features were viewed individually and the frescoes served as gap fillers. In *chhatris* this was very rare, because of the clear-cut spherical area of the interior of the dome which made it possible to see everything at once. The subject could be, for example, the complete *Ramayana*, as on the ceiling of a *chhatri* at Ramgarh, or just one scene, such as the wedding of Rama and Sita, which may be seen at Chirawa *(Plate 47)*.

THE RELIGIOUS CONTENT

The *kula devata*, or patron deity, of the Shekhavat Rajputs is Gopinath-ji, that is, Krishna in his amorous aspect as Lord of the *Gopis*, or Milkmaids. The Marwaris, also, have a natural reverence for Krishna. Thus in Rajput forts, in Marwari houses and in the temples of both communities, Krishna-*gopi* episodes dominate the Shekhavati frescoes. Those appearing most frequently are *vastra harana*, the story of Krishna carrying off the *gopis'* clothes while they are bathing *(Plate 60)*; *rasa mandala*, the cosmic circular dance of Krishna in which he multiplies himself to be with every *gopi*, and so representing the incarnation of the eternal principle in the universe *(Plate 60)*; and the incident in which Indra, the God of Rain, lets loose a torrential shower on

the herders and Krishna comes to their rescue by lifting the entire Govardhana mountain so that it shelters them like an umbrella *(Plate 64)*. Besides these clichés of the Krishna-*gopi* theme is *narikunjara*, an amalgam of milkmaids to form a horse *(cover)*, an elephant *(Plate 62)*, a palanquin (as in the *Soné Chandi ki haveli* at Mahansar), or a swing on which Krishna sits. Rarely, an erotic representation of this subject may be found. Another interesting Krishna form is *navakunjara*, a fantastic creature created from a combination of animals, some of which are symbolic of Krishna. *Navakunjara* is usually composed of a peacock's head, a human hand holding the *gada*, or war mace, of Vishnu, a horse's fore-leg, the hind legs of a tiger and an elephant, a snake's tail and a bull's body. When this supernatural creature is shown with Krishna's head, the peacock may appear on his crown. Somewhere a camel's head or hump or the wings of an eagle are represented, depending on the fancy of the artist. Folk artists were forever seeking new, ingenious ways of representing traditional stories from mythology. Their favourite Krishna legends have now had some twenty centuries of expression, both in art and in literature, and thousands of versions have emerged.

In the Shekhavati frescoes, other Krishna legends are also popular: Krishna subduing the serpent-king Kaliya while his mermaid-wives plead with folded hands for their master's life to be spared; Krishna taking the wicked King Kamsa by his hair and dragging him from the throne to the arena where he is slain; Krishna fighting the elephant-demon Kuvalayapida.

The Shekhavat Rajputs are Kachhawahas, and the temple of their *kula devata*, Jamvai Mata, is near Jaipur, close to the Ramgarh lake where their ancestor Dulérai-ji of Dausa defeated the local Meenas. To this day all the Kachhawahas pay their respects to Jamvai Mata. In Jaipur the Gopinath-ji temple most sacred to the Shekhavats is near Chandpol.

In his search for a rationale for the tremendous popular following that Krishna has spontaneously drawn from all over India, Francis G. Hutchins propounds an interesting theory:

> A person named Krishna probably lived in northern India about three thousand years ago, and probably took part as one among many noble chieftains in the great dynastic war which forms the subject of the twenty-five-hundred-year-old epic poem the *Mahabharata*. Then, about two thousand years ago, Krishna came to be thought of increasingly as the principal human incarnation of the god Vishnu and hence a definitive enunciator of religious truth.

He points out that even Akbar called attention to the Krishna texts to circumvent contemporary Hindu dogmatists, and at the same time to neutralize ill-informed Muslim criticism of Krishna's followers. In terms of continuity, too, this had far-reaching effects: the painters who returned from the Mughal ateliers had not become alienated from their own traditions.

This Vaishnavite following among the inhabitants of Shekhavati which began from Krishna, the eighth incarnation of Vishnu, went on to the *dasavataras* – the ten incarnations of Vishnu. This theme neatly lent itself for painting in the panels between the stone brackets supporting the overhanging rooms and balconies. Since the worship of Rama-Sita is common among the Marwaris, the scenes from the *Ramayana* also appear frequently in the frescoes.

The Shekhavat Rajputs worship Hanuman, the monkey god, whom they call Bala-ji. He appears at the centre of their triangular flag, and his worship is said to bring good luck in war. Before going into battle the Rajputs invoked Shakti, the female symbol of energy, and before embarking on a journey, even today, they commonly worship Bala-ji, or Hanuman. The Marwaris, before travelling, worship *devis*, or goddesses, which are the favourite of their immediate clan. These *ishta devis* are also invoked on auspicious occasions and festivals, and once a year the Marwaris go out on a pilgrimage to the sites of the *devi* temples. (*Devis*, also known as *matas*, represent the mother goddess.) The more popular ones in Shekhavati are Jeen Mata, a sixth-century temple at Jeen, near Gorian; Rani Sati, a temple at Jhunjhunu built in 1934 to immortalize a Marwari lady who burnt herself on her husband's pyre; Sham-ji, at Khatu; Sikrai, at Koth Sikrai near Udaipurvati; and Sakambari, near the Balsana-Ringus hills. The people of Shekhavati also worship at the Hanuman temple at Salasar, near Sikar, believing that this helps to solve mental disorders.

The Marwaris take particular care to worship Lakshmi, the Goddess of Wealth, who is the consort of Vishnu the Preserver. On the festival of Diwali, hundreds of oil lamps are lit along the path by which Lakshmi is expected to enter the house, for it is believed that the Goddess of Wealth does not come through a dark portal.

Unlike South India, where Vaishnavite-Shivaite demarcations are rigid among the Hindus, in Shekhavati the followers of Vishnu worship Shiva and Shakti with equal ease. Such Hindus are called *Smarta*. The worship of Shiva is more popular among the Rajput *thakurs*. The womenfolk worship the goddess Gangor, a manifestation of Gauri whose consort, Isar-ji, is himself a manifestation of Shiva. To unmarried women Gangor worship can mean a good husband and family; to the married, continued marital bliss.

Ganesha, the elephant-headed son of Shiva, appears unfailingly at the entrance of every house in Shekhavati, often more than once. His image is intricately carved on the wooden lintel, seated contentedly on a mouse, and attended on both sides by his wives Riddhi and Siddhi (the means and the end). Ganesha's image is sometimes carved on a block of stone which is set into the wall; it may also be made in lime plaster relief or painted in fresco. Since this image is worshipped by applying saffron, it shows up bright and luminous on the brown of the wood or against the white walls.

In Shekhavati as in some other parts of India, *pitra puja*, or ancestor worship, is quite common. In the inner courtyard of the *havelis* a painted niche, called *pitar-ji ko mandh*, is devoted to the worship of forefathers, who are considered *griha devatas*, or guardian spirits of the home. This worship of the *veera*, or hero, is more widespread in Western and Central India, though it is also practised in the north.

Indra, the God of Rain, is worshipped particularly when the monsoon fails. On such an occasion a ritual is performed around a fire and all the communities participate. *Agni*, or fire, is itself considered holy: every day the first *roti* (round bread, prepared on a hot plate) cooked in the kitchen is offered to the flames, for each time the fire is lit the God of Fire is born anew. Some people presumably feeling this to be a waste, prefer to give it to a dog.

THE COLONIAL INFLUENCE

If the earlier frescoes dealt mostly with religious and traditional themes, the later frescoes tackled a broader spectrum. They were influenced by oleographs, lithographs and photographs from England, and also, in particular, by the work of Raja Ravi Verma of Travancore (1848–1906). It is amusing to note that while Ravi Verma's work was new and in a way un-Indian, in 1893 the World's Columbian Commission in Chicago, honoured his 'exhibit of ten paintings', declaring them 'of much ethnological value'. Of his 'salon-type academicism', Geeta Kapur writes:

> . . . that obsolete and much derided artist Raja Ravi Verma, the first Indian to gain acclaim in oil painting . . . put all the faith and fervour of a new convert into the newly imported medium of oils, and he used its inherently sumptuous qualities to give his mythological figures an extra appeal by modelling them, highlighting the scene, giving an overall gloss to the picture. In turn, the urbanised patrons, from the aristocracy to the ever widening middle class, responded positively to these new-fangled effects, and the demand for Ravi Verma's paintings increased so rapidly that the technique of oleographic printing was introduced in India to mass-produce his paintings.

When these oleographs arrived in Shekhavati the obvious happened: they became the fashion of the day, both with the patrons and with the artists, who were instantly seduced by their gloss. The next stage saw them transferred to the walls as frescoes (*Plates 73 and 74*). The artists already had access to the hybrid paintings, that evolved after the British arrived, in which Indian miniatures crossed with the naturalism of Western paintings to produce some curious results. This new school of painting was branded the Company School, after the East India Company. It flourished from 1760 to about 1880, after which the hybridization was complete, and its peculiarities were incorporated into the Indian mainstream.

Photography came to India in the 1840s. In the cities, the artists were slowly replaced by photographers. (In the late 1840s the New Calcutta Directory listed four professional portrait painters active in Calcutta. By the 1850s not one was listed.) But in the smaller towns and in the villages where the camera itself took longer to arrive, photographs became models for the artists to paint from. On the walls of Shekhavati there are European portraits painted from photographs: Queen-Empress Victoria, George V and Queen Mary, English gentlemen riding bicycles, much-bejewelled ladies with low necklines, and many others.

Portraits of kings, wealthy merchants, warriors, and so on, often cover a series of rectangular frames on a wall. Portraits of men were much larger in number, no doubt reflecting the narcissism and vanity of a male-dominated society. Women made few and discreet appearances, unless they were from mythology or folklore in which case they needed no social approval.

The frescoes, which may have begun as decoration, gradually developed into a status symbol. Slowly, as the merchants migrated, the hinterland was deserted for the ports and cities that offered better business opportunities. And as the merchants prospered they sent their wealth home. Gradually, the Marwari mansions in Shekhavati started competing with each other, growing in size and increasing in ornamentation.

At the ports, the Marwaris outdid the rest and equalled the British in commercial success. Soon it was time to imitate the rulers' tastes. Their dwelling places, back in their villages and towns, began to wear the *nouveau riche* façade. The mansions that arose were grand, and later became pompous and decadent. The fresco race was on. Frescoes were now not so much the mark of a patron of the arts as they were a way of displaying wealth. 'Twenty artists worked for two years in our *haveli*, staying and eating at our cost,' boasted the lady of the house, and the word went round the neighbourhood.

To emulate the British was to rise in the social hierarchy. This worked for the content of the frescoes as well: motor cars were now more elegant than elephants, angels more aesthetic than local gods. A new phase had begun: the indigenous was replaced by the European. Strolling *barra sahibs* and *memsahibs** were painted on the façades of houses, their pet dogs tied on a leash. Clumsy trains and cars drawn from imagination carried wealthy Marwaris. Alien subjects like aeroplanes, sailing ships and telephones covered the walls of mansions between 1880 and 1930.

Herman Goetz, commenting on a similar transformation of tastes in the neighbouring state of Bikaner, wrote, 'At present the tradition is rapidly degenerating ... Houses are decorated with copies of pseudo-Gothic scroll work and grotesque "portraits" of Queen Victoria, Edward VII etc...'.

Earlier, the foreigner had been the *sudra 'Feringhee'*, the low-caste alien. 'A prince would not eat in the same pot', Colonel James Tod, the eminent English historian, writes, 'because earthenware could not be purified'. But now British residents had walked in to govern and administer. Rajput pride, which had been boundless, had no choice but to bow to a stronger military force. This subservience was reflected in the frescoes.

A major change in the content of the frescoes had come about before the turn of the century *(Plate 84)*. The 'Great Jeypore Exhibition' of 1883, which took place in the Albert Hall† in the Ram Niwas Garden, had far-reaching effects. Organized by Surgeon Major T. H. Hendley, the exhibition displayed many European objects – books, atlases, lithographs, etchings and engravings – as well as a collection of Indian objects. The exhibition contributed to a broader intercourse between the two different cultures, and Shekhavati, in the immediate neighbourhood, was quick to mirror the changes.

This exposure of the secluded desert States to influences from the West had both interesting and unfortunate results. Many indigenous traditions began to fall apart. The beauty and relevance of the local dress, for example, was threatened by the European attire better suited to a colder climate. It became fashionable to associate oneself with Western inventions such as the motor car and the train. Although the first train entered Shekhavati in 1916, (the 'Jeypore-Sheikhawati branch' that ran from Ringus to Jhunjhunu), there were many lopsided versions of it in the frescoes that had preceded it by three or four decades. Several of these show that the painters had let their imaginations run wild. Some painted horses inside the engine, others managed to fit just two people into a whole bogey. A relatively educated Bengali who had obviously had some exposure to the British and to the trains they had brought, still tended to treat a public train as a private carriage. The following letter, written to the 'white' transportation superintendent, dated 2 July 1909, describes the interaction of two cultures, and a transition that was both sad and amusing:

Dear Sir:
I am arrive by passenger train at Ahmedpur station and my belly is too much swelling with jackfruit. I am therefore went to privy. Just as I doing the nuisance that guard making whistle blow for train to go off and I am running with *lotah* [water pot] in one hand and *dhoti* in the next when I am fall over and expose all my shocking to man, female, women on platform. I am get leaved at Ahmedpur station.

This too much bad if passenger go to make dung that dam guard no wait train five minutes for him. I am therefore pray your honour to make big fine on that guard for public sake. Otherwise I am making big report to papers.
Yours faithful servant
Okhil Ch. Sen.

The colonizing yoke brutalized many of the ethnic values. Combined with this was a lingering feudalism. The hangover of these had drained what Geeta Kapur calls 'the plenitude of imagination out of which a people fashion their identity'. As an extension of this complex, the man on the street now disowns the frescoes and admires the transistor radios and watches that are infiltrating his village.

* Words coined during the British rule to address Englishmen and their wives, still used by servants to address their Indian 'masters' and 'mistresses'.

† Albert Hall had been designed by Sir Swinton Jacob, the State engineer of Jaipur, for the visit of Prince Edward.

Death or revival?

THE FIRST WORLD WAR had moved some Marwaris to industry, and by the Second World War they were urbanized enough not to want to return to their villages and towns. For them the cities had now become their dwelling places.

In the *havelis*, caretakers' families now huddle in a single room, taking little care of the mansion. Smoke from their fires blackens the painted walls. The other rooms are locked up or vacant. Those who come – an old man driven by childhood nostalgia, a groom to show the ancestral home to his bride or to make an offering at the patron deity's shrine – stay for a day or two and then leave. Otherwise, little happens beyond the teashop gatherings and the market transactions, the games of cards and *chaupar**, the chewing of the betel leaf, the smoking of the hookah. In the middle of this stillness a bus may arrive raising dust and rousing the lazy from their endless siestas. A donkey-cart may pass through a painted street. Now and then, camels will stride past the desert-brown walls, their awkward humps blending with the dunes beyond.

The land has not been bounteous in Shekhavati; but, ironically, this has proved advantageous. The sons of this arid soil, reared in austerity, have gone out to seek their own fortunes, and have brought home the bounties of other lands. Even today, the land depends on the whims of the clouds – the Rajasthan Canal remains a distant dream. Shekhavati's inhabitants retain their migratory pattern. Thousands are lured by the lucrative prospects in the Middle East, where factories, construction sites, hotels, transport and trading companies absorb the new migrants.

After a lull in the 1930s, money is once again flowing into Shekhavati, but with different results. The crisp, coloured cottons have been overtaken by nylons and acrylics, synthetic shoes have replaced the leather *jooties*†. The new houses are garish and conspicuous; the temples have mirrors and multi-coloured tiles; mosques with blaring loudspeakers invite the faithful to prayer. Tradition is disowned; instant prosperity shows only its *nouveau riche* façades; some frescoed walls get a coat of plastic emulsion. Since there is little regard for the old, there is no effort at renovation and repair. Even though most of the frescoed *havelis* belong to a community that continues to have the means, the towns of Shekhavati have the semblance of crumbling ghost settlements.

On his visit to the court of Jahangir, the Mughal emperor, an early seventeenth-century Dutch traveller had noted:

> Nothing is permanent ... once a builder is dead, no one will care for the buildings; the son will neglect the father's work, the mother her son's, brothers and friends will take no care for each other's buildings; everyone tries, as far as possible, to erect a new building of his own, and establish his own reputation alongside that of his ancestors. Consequently, it may be said that if all these buildings and erections were attended to and repaired for a century, the lands of every city, and even village, would be adorned with monuments; but, as a matter of fact, the roads leading to the cities are strewn with fallen columns of stone.

In Shekhavati, the truth of this statement can hardly be more telling and unfortunate.

* A local dice game likened to the Chinese ludo, played on a chequered, cross-shaped cloth with three long ivory *pasas* (dice) and sixteen *shayars* (pawns).

† A closed, pointed shoe without laces, normally worn by villagers.

THE PLATES

All measurements are in centimetres:
height precedes width.

2 A frescoed *haveli*, or mansion, typical of Shekhavati. The painted walls show some of the popular themes: horses, elephants, portraits, ladies flying kites. *Havelis* such as these were the homes of the mercantile class, the Marwaris, who traded along the caravan routes in opium, salt, indigo, grain and cloth. These merchants later migrated to the ports and business centres for brokerage, trading and speculation. Thomas A. Timberg observes, 'Today it is estimated that more than half the assets in the modern sector of the Indian economy are controlled by the trading castes originating in the northern half of Rajasthan'.

Haveli of Kaneh Ram Narsingh Das Tibdiwala in Jhunjhunu. Built in 1883.

I Cows pass before the *haveli* of the Birlas, the richest family in India. It is said that Ganesh Narayan-ji, a famous saint of Chirawa, impressed by the piety and devotion of a certain Baldeodas, had blessed him with prosperity. Baldeodas, later titled 'Raja' Baldeodas by the British goverment, was to become the founder of the Birla empire. His son Seth Jugal Kishore (the elder brother of the present head of the family Ghanshyam Das Birla) was given the title of Raja by Maharaja Man Singh of Jaipur.

  The Birla family now lives in the cities, while the ancestral *haveli* houses a small museum.

Façade of the Shiv Narayan Birla haveli in Pilani. Built in 1864.

3 Painted arches beside the main entrance of a *haveli*. Houses built on this pattern normally had three decorative arches on each side of the entrance *(page 24)*. The arches here carry portraits of men seated on ornamental chairs. Their postures are comparable to those seen in the formal photographs of the second half of the nineteenth century. The fan, the gun, the umbrella, the walking stick and the hubble bubble – suggestive of leisure – were symbols of men of position.

Detail from the façade of the Krishan Mahan Prasad Rathi haveli in Lachhmangarh. Built around 1890.
200 × 260 cm.

4 A Rajasthani lady peeps from behind her *ghungat* or veil. It was not customary for women to show their faces, a practice prevalent till today in traditional families.

The women remained in the *zenana*, the ladies' apartments, and had only an occasional glimpse of the man's world through their veils or through intricately latticed windows. Such was the pride of a Rajput that no man dare set an eye on his woman.

'To the fair of the other lands, the fate of a *Rajputni* must appear one of appalling hardship. In each stage of life, death is ready to claim her,' wrote Lieutenant-Colonel Tod in the early nineteenth century: 'female infanticide at birth, *jauhar* or mass immolation in case of defeat in war, and *sati* or self immolation on becoming a widow.'

Here the lady of the house is seen with all her silver jewellery: rings, bangles, armlets, anklets, toe-rings and silver chains, from one of which dangles a bunch of keys. She wears a *kanchali*, a short blouse that covers only half the breast. Her skirt is printed in *bandhani*, a process of tying and dyeing whereby the colour escapes the tied portions. In her hand she holds a *punkha*, or fan, made with straw and frilled with cloth.

Fresco in the courtyard of the Kesar Dev Saraf haveli in Lachhmangarh. Built around 1880. 100 × 65 cm.

5 In their days of glory the *havelis*, much like the palaces, had their own guards. Today, time has seen them retreat into the walls. The painted versions that flank the entrances have different costumes, headgear and weapons, representative of the varied traditions brought by the artists.

This tradition of protecting the entrance goes back to the early temples where *dikapalas* guarded the eight directions of space and *dwarapalas* (male guardians) or *dwara balahis* (female guardians) carved in stone or wood stood watch on either side of the gateways.

FROM LEFT TO RIGHT: *guards painted on havelis in Churi Ajitgarh (1918), Chirawa (1929), and Lachhmangarh (1979). On average, these guards are 100 cm high.*

6 The costumes introduced by the British well matched the regalia of the Rajput courts. Colourful sashes in the puggarees, braided pipings, gilded cummerbunds, jodhpurs, polished brass buttons and epaulettes – all demonstrated the imperial pageantry of a power at the height of its glory. The *kulledar* puggaree, worn here by the soldier on the left, was a turban of Pathan origin, introduced by the British for their police forces.

Detail of a 6-metre-long fresco on the Manohar Lal Vaid haveli in Chirawa. Built around 1929. The figures are 90 cm high.

38

7

Krishna, the most popular deity in India, is the master of *maya*, or illusion. Above this portal, in his *rasa mandala*, or cosmic circular dance, Krishna manifests his omnipresence.

Two carved Ganeshas, one on the wooden lintel and another below the arch, ensure an auspicious entry into the house. This pot-bellied, elephant-headed God of the Portal sits on a mouse. Worshipped before undertaking any new venture, he is supposed to remove all obstacles, The three hangings are called *torans*, each one symbolizing the wedding of a daughter of the house.

Entrance arch of the Kripa Ram Dhuramka (now called Jhunjhunwala) haveli in Mukundgarh. Built in 1859.

8 Two Rajputs (literally sons of princes), who are the descendants of the warrior clans, sit on a rope cot and chat in the courtyard of a *haveli*. The saffron of their turbans was the traditional colour worn during wartime. The man on the right holds a *barchhi*, a self-defence weapon.

Most *havelis* in Shekhavati have one courtyard at the entrance and an inner courtyard where the ladies remain and carry on their daily chores. Above the door are two carved idols of Ganesha. Perhaps this is what makes him the most widely worshipped deity of the Hindu pantheon. Flanking the carved Ganeshas, and on both sides of the door, are his wives Riddhi and Siddhi, the 'means' and the 'end'. Above the carved door are portraits of gods, covered with glass and interspersed with mirror-work.

The inner gate of the Mohan Ram Ishwar Das Modi haveli in Jhunjhunu. Built in 1896.

9 A fish-eye view of a *haveli*. Built by two brothers, it was later divided by their progeny by building a wall through the common courtyard. The elliptical arches painted on this *haveli* harmoniously lead to the foliated entrance arches on both sides. Every inch of wall surface is worked with equal attention, the shape of the larger frescoes cleverly manipulated to avoid the windows. A linear panel of portraits, above the horses and elephants, is executed with the precision of miniature paintings. The stone brackets, the wooden doors and windows match the exuberance of the frescoes.

Façade of the Ladhuram Tarkeshwar Goenka haveli in Mandawa. Built around 1870.

10 The windows of the *havelis* were nearly always small, to keep out the heat and dust. This architecture also suited the lifestyle of the women, who were supposed to remain in the privacy of the house. Doors from all the rooms led to the courtyard or, on the first floor, to balconies which overlooked the courtyard, thus solving the problem of light from the inside. The open patch of sky also countered the claustrophobia of the rooms. In some *havelis*, small ventilators above the windows were fixed with wood or stone *jalis*, or latticed grilles, and left open for air circulation. In others, these were closed with coloured glass, so that the light which entered the rooms was delicately tinted.

11 A detail of the windows shows the extent to which artists went while painting the frescoes. Each tableau between and above the *todis*, or stone brackets, carries a complete painting.

Side view and detail of the Dedraj Tormal Bhudarmal Goenka haveli in Mandawa. Built in 1898.

I2 In this detail from a series of windows, exquisitely painted oval medallions show Indians and Europeans. The former hold flowers or birds, while the latter hold guns. Three portraits on the left show Englishmen on bicycles.

Windows of the Puran Mal Chiranji Lal Chhawchhariya haveli in Nawalgarh. Built around 1875. The four windows measure 5 metres across.

13 Painted on the wall of this courtyard is a scene of Gajalakshmi, the Goddess of Wealth, who sits on a lotus adored by two ranks of elephants. Lakshmi, the wife of Vishnu the Preserver and mother of Kama, the God of Love, was supposedly born from the foam of the ocean.

 Under the frescoes, a man renovates the ruined floor.

Courtyard of the Jagannath Singhania haveli in Fatehpur. Built around 1870.

14 Girls in the courtyard of the Birla *haveli* shell *kair*, the pods of which are similar in appearance to those of the laburnum. These are plucked from stunted desert shrubs and made into pickles. Members of the Birla family who now live in the cities have not given up their taste for *kair*, and have it collected for them.

 Although a part of the back wall has been whitewashed, the original frescoes are preserved and seem to stand out in relief. Between the painted brackets are scenes of cavaliers, soldiers, and merchants, while the upper portions carry floral designs.

Courtyard of the Shiv Narayan Birla haveli in Pilani. Built in 1864.

16

Gilded portraits of Indians (above) and Europeans (below) painted on the ceiling of a verandah (facing page). The Indian lady is shown praying with a rosary, her hand inside a *gaumukhi*, a cloth bag shaped like the head of a cow. In the other hand she holds a *morchhal*, a fan of peacock feathers. A receptacle for holy water and other objects of prayer lie on a *chauki*, or low table, in the background. Her transparent muslin blouse is much like the Mughal paintings of the sixteenth century. The Indian man with a gilded stick is probably the Mughal emperor Jahangir. This Muslim influence can be attributed to the large Muslim population of Fatehpur which was ruled by the Kayamkhani nawabs until AD 1512.

The European lady petting her lap-dog is seen with the differences in costume that must have appealed to the artist: the ribboned hat, the turned cuff, the rather masculine coat. It is obvious from the armlets and the hairstyle that the artist had little knowledge of how English ladies looked or what they wore. The European man, probably a soldier, also carries on him what were supposedly the attributes of a foreigner: a bottle, a gun and a hat.

It is interesting to note that the Indian and European faces have a keen resemblance.

Fish-eye view and details of frescoes from Nand Lal Devra's haveli in Fatehpur. Built around 1890. The ovals measure 60 × 39 cm.

15 A fish-eye view of the *tibari*, or three-arched verandah, showing gilded portraits. A carved wooden beam divides the ceiling into two with twelve painted medallions on each side. The central space is decorated with mirrors, golden strappings and an elaborate pattern of flowers and fruits.

Normally this area was used as a *baithak*, literally a 'sitting', where the men of the house conducted their business. Large cotton mattresses were placed on the floor and covered with white sheets. Bulky white bolsters served as back rests. Visitors removed their shoes on entering the *haveli* and sat cross-legged on the mattresses. Perhaps it was this absence of furniture that encouraged the profusion of ornamentation.

17 A camel passes before Nagar Mal Somani's *haveli* in Islampur. The scene in the background is a detail from the famous Rajasthani romance of Dhola and Maru. Built in 1880, this fortress-like *haveli* earned itself the name 'Chittorgarh' after the impregnable fort of Rana Pratap of Udaipur.

'Dhola-Maru', the most popular folk legend of Rajasthan, tells an unusual love story. Once upon a time there was a famine in Poongal, near Jaisalmer. Rao Pingal, the ruler of Poongal, moved to Narwar, near Gwalior, where he was well received by Raja Nal. There, Rao Pingal's daughter, Maru, who was a year and a half old, was married to Dhola, who was Raja Nal's three-year-old son.

After the famine, Rao Pingal returned to Poongal with his family. Many years passed, and Raja Nal re-married Dhola to the Princess of Malwa.

Meanwhile, Maru had come of age, but Dhola never came to take her home. Messages to Dhola were intercepted by his new bride and the messengers killed. But one day, two folk singers came to Dhola's palace and sang him the sad message of the pining Maru. Dhola grew angry and impatient to see his childhood wife, and the singers were handsomely rewarded.

While Dhola yearned to bring Maru to his palace, his second wife kept close guard on him throughout the summer and monsoon. One stormy night in autumn, Dhola escaped on a camel while his wife was asleep. On the way he met Oomar Soomra, whose marriage proposals to Maru had been refused. Oomar discouraged Dhola: 'Why do you go to Maru? She is an old hag now.' But Dhola was determined to reach her. When he arrived at Poongal, he was welcomed with great ceremony. He stayed for fifteen days, and then, with Maru, left for home on camel-back. But on the way Maru died of a snake bite. Beside himself with grief, Dhola built a pyre for his beloved and planned to burn himself with her. But before this could happen, Shiva and his wife Parvati passed by, disguised as ascetics. Parvati pleaded with Shiva to put life into Maru. Shiva did so, and Dhola and Maru continued on their journey home.

They were then followed by the jealous Oomar Soomra, who planned to kidnap Maru. But a maidservant let out the plot. Dhola and Maru escaped on their camel and reached Narwar safely. The other wife joined them, and the three lived happily together.

The scene most often represented in the Dhola-Maru frescoes shows them fleeing on camel-back from the army of Oomar Soomra. Maru, who is always seated behind, defends them both by shooting arrows or firing at the army with a gun.

18 Three men of position ride a carriage drawn by two camels. Two of them sit face to face smelling flowers, while the third holds a dagger. Seated on the floorboard are two children, who share with the adults a love for pet birds. It was the constraint of the space under the window that possibly prompted the artist to draw children instead of adults.

Fresco on the Sanwatram Chokhani haveli in Lachhmangarh. Built around 1860. 140 × 300 cm.

20 A life-sized elephant painted on the façade of a *haveli*. Near the trunk of the elephant is the 'DDT' marking of the National Malaria Eradication Programme. Every house disinfected under this scheme carries this graffiti near its entrance. The tapestry and garments, executed in great detail, give the semblance of rich fabric, as in miniature paintings. The two noblemen in the centre smell flowers and hold swords while their attendants wave the *chamvar*, or ceremonial fly-whisk.

A traveller in the second century of our era reported: 'The animals used by the common sort for riding on are camels and horses and asses, while the wealthy use elephants – for it is the elephant which in India carries royalty. The conveyance which ranks next in honour is the chariot; the camel ranks third; while to be drawn by a single horse is considered no distinction at all.'

Fresco on the Sukhdev Das Ganeriwala haveli in Mukundgarh, now belonging to the Kanorias. Built around 1880. 275 × 400 cm.

19 A bejewelled elephant with ornamented tusks being driven by a Muslim *mahout*. This Muslim influence can be attributed to the Nagar Pathans who ruled Baggar from 1456 until 1732, when they were driven away by Shekhavat Hindu Rajputs. A mixture of styles can also be seen in the eyes of the elephant: even though he is painted in profile, both eyes are visible. This is in the tradition of Jain manuscripts of the fifteenth century and of early miniature paintings.

The ventilation holes above the elephant's head are blackened by smoke.

Detail from a fresco on the Swaroop Chand Prithviraj Rungta haveli in Baggar. Built around 1850. 200 × 130 cm.

51

21 A three-trunked elephant, probably a variation of Airavata, the three-trunked white elephant of Indra, the God of Rain. In one of the trunks the elephant carries a whisk to assist the *mahout* in keeping flies off the rider. Seated on the *howdah*, or elephant seat, is a four-armed divinity, probably of local origin. Bells at the bottom tinkle with every stride as the *mahout* controls the animal with an *ankush*, or elephant goad.

A fresco from the Puran Mal Chiranji Lal Chhawchhariya haveli in Nawalgarh. Built around 1875. 200 × 150 cm.

22 A multi-storeyed carriage called *Indra Viman*, or the vehicle of Indra drawn by two elephants. A similar carriage was used by Sawai Jai Singh, the Maharaja of Jaipur, to inspect his 'pink city' after its completion in 1727.

Fresco from the Sanwatram Chokhani haveli in Lachhmangarh. Built around 1860. 220 × 330 cm.

23 A large elephant walks across a wall. On the top left is a lady playing with a yo-yo and on the right another plays a *vina* (a musical instrument with several strings and gourds as resonators). The symmetry of the composition is maintained at the bottom with a camel rider on the left and a horseman to the right – now ruined by an election slogan. The colours, though limited to reds, browns and greens, create a spectacular effect.

At the bottom, impressions of painted hands called *thapas* are a present-day symbolism of the practice of *sati.* Widows who mounted the funeral pyres of their husbands, and supposedly became goddesses, are remembered by commemorative tablets of their hand prints. Some women threw themselves wilfully into the fire, mad with grief, others had to be persuaded to do so for reasons of family honour. Although the British declared this practice illegal in the early nineteenth century, *satis* in Shekhavati have been recorded in the twentieth century: in 1934 at Jhunjhunu, in 1972 at Lohargal. Temples now mark the sites of their sacrifice.

Fresco on the Motilal Bhotika haveli in Fatehpur. Built around 1850. 300 × 430 cm.

24 Biographical frescoes on the ceiling of Shardul Singh's cremation *chhatri*, built by his wife Mertani-ji in *1750 (see also page 15 and Plate 42)*. In its mortuary aspect the *chhatri* often took the shape of a grand cenotaph. After Shardul Singh's death at Parasrampura, his five sons became heirs to Jhunjhunu. The Maharaja of Jodhpur requested them through an emissary not to divide the land, but to no avail. Five equal shares were given to the sons, who came to be called the Panchpanas. The law of primogeniture had been abolished because it had led to so many fraternal squabbles, and henceforth property was equally divided among all the sons. However, a sub-caste in Shekhavati, known as the *Bhojraj-ji-ka*, still maintain primogeniture.

Painted interior of the dome of Shardul Singh's cenotaph in Parasrampura. Built in 1750.

25 A detail from Shardul Singh's *chhatri* shows a skewbald horse, or *ablak*, bedecked with all his finery. This horse, much superior to the others painted on the ceiling of this dome, would probably have been Shardul's very own.

While a horse's mane was left open to fly in the wind, a mare's mane was braided with long silken tassels. *Jhools*, or long, swinging pompons, dangled between the legs for beauty.

Shalihotra, the ancient Hindu treatise on horses by Nala, leaves out no detail on the variety of horses, their selection; training, diet, treatment, etc.

Horses' colours are commonly compared with those of pigeons. The latter are reported to have one more colour than the horses.

Detail from Shardul Singh's chhatri in Parasrampura. Built in 1750.

26 The powerful bird Anarpankh carrying a mythical beast likened to Shardul, a tiger-like beast. A similar bird is called Udbakavali. Other cultures also have fantastic birds: Simurgh, the Persian bird of revelation, carries elephants which symbolize the inferior elements of the individual 'Me'; in the Japanese Ho-o or Phoenix, the elephants are replaced by a dragon. The supreme bird of Indian mythology is Garuda, the king of the woods and the vehicle of Vishnu, the Preserver, and his wife Lakshmi, the Goddess of Wealth.

Detail from Shardul Singh's cremation chhatri in Parasrampura. Built in 1750.

27 Colourful frescoes on the façade of a *haveli* stand out against the sand of the desert. Pupul Jayakar comments on man's necessity to counter the colourlessness of nature: 'The great colour belt in the west stretches from Baluchistan and Sindh through the deserts of Kathiawar, Rajasthan and Gujarat; it was as if the arid wasteland of the desert, the gnarled babul tree, the fierce noon-day and the absence of green in the landscape, demanded the recompense of colour...'.

Façade of the Sneh Ram Harmukh Rai Chokhani haveli in Mandawa. Built in 1905.

58

29 A proud cavalier rides his caparisoned horse. Since the Rajputs took great pride in their horses it was natural for them to keep their animals healthy and well adorned. The fresco here shows the decorative *jaal* which was much like the *gorband*, the festive neckgear for camels. The style of the *safa*, or turban, worn by the rider was first introduced by Sir Pertap of Idar who fought for the British in the Boer War.

The tribulte of Colonel J. C. Brooks in his *Political History of Jaipur* could hardly have been an overstatement: 'There is no recruiting ground for cavalry in India at all equal to Shekhawati'.

Detail of a fresco from the haveli of Hariram Ram Prasad Sahal, in Nawalgarh. Built in 1901. 50 × 70 cm.

28 A Rajput showed his riding skill by making his horse gallop after a slow walk. From a full gallop he could again make the animal walk, eliminating the trot and the canter.

In this fresco of a galloping blue horse, the artist displays his ingenuity in the use of space, incorporating the window as a part of the design.

Fresco on the Dedraj Tormal Bhudarmal Goenka haveli in Mandawa. Built in 1898. 200 × 90 cm.

30 Two cavaliers, one with a spear and the other with a gun, walk their horses in step. Rajput warriors were essentially cavaliers, and it was not unusual for them to look down on foot soldiers. There are many instances since the days of the *Mahabharata* when horse worship was performed and wars waged over horses. The relative importance of this noble animal can hardly be expressed more explicitly than in the words of the Hara Prince of Bundi who is reported to have told the Lodi King at Delhi, 'There are three things you must not ask a Rajput: his horse; his mistress or his sword.'

The peeled plaster reveals the rough wall surface prepared for the lime. The process of *arayish*, or lime work, was tedious. Pure stone lime was dissolved in water and then strained. This was mixed with pulverized white marble and applied wet to the wall, which was then rubbed smooth with a polished stone. A second coating of the paste was applied and burnished with agate. The design was then drawn on the prepared wall by rubbing powdered charcoal through a perforated stencil. The colouring followed rapidly, while the plaster-coated surface was still moist. Finally the wall was washed with coconut water and burnished with agate.

Detail from the façade of the Hari Baksh Saraf haveli in Mandawa. Built in 1906. 160 × 200 cm.

31 This fresco of a *shikar*, or hunt, shows a Rajput firing from his horse. Amusingly enough, the bird seems a willing prey. To shoot at a moving target from a galloping horse must have been a difficult feat, but then the Rajputs prided themselves at being crack shots.

In later years some Britons adopted this sport. Others used the horse purely for recreational riding, for inspection tours of remote places, and for the odd *chukker* of polo. Charles Allen writes: 'It was the horse that made possible such genteel entertainment as the gymkhana and the Saturday morning paperchase ... and such bizarre blood sports as jackal hunting ... and pig sticking!'

The Maharaja of Bharatpur, in Rajasthan, created a waterbird shooting resort which became very popular among the British Viceroys. The most memorable hunt was that of Lord Linlithgow, in 1938, who shot 1900 rounds. He and his party of thirty-nine guns gathered a record bag of 4273 birds.

Fresco on the Dedraj Tormal Bhudarmal Goenka haveli in Mandawa. Built in 1898. 200 × 90 cm.

32 A tiger *shikar*, or hunt, on elephant back. It was considered more adventurous and gallant to shoot from elephant-back than from the treetop *machan*, since the hunter was more vulnerable to the attack. In this fresco, the tiger is seen leaping on the elephant while the riders try to spear him and to shoot arrows. A dog in the background, probably an artist's version of a hound, simultaneously attacks the tiger. By the late nineteenth century it was common for the British and the Maharajas to import hounds for their *shikar*.

Detail from a fresco on the Umrao Singh Dalmia haveli in Chirawa. Built around 1895. 100 × 120 cm.

33 A detail of two horsemen hunting wild boar. Deftness and skill on horseback were important qualifications for a Rajput. Sons of Rajputs were trained for war from the age of six: riding, hunting, archery, fencing and, later, shooting were the games of their childhood. At twelve they were considered fit for the battlefield and at fourteen were married and treated as adults.

Warfare was particularly important to the Rajputs, not just for fighting invading armies but during wars of succession and other petty skirmishes that often arose between the chieftains.

Detail of a fresco on the Sanwatram Chokhani haveli in Lachhmangarh. Built around 1860. 200 × 150 cm.

34 A scene from an *akhara*, or an arena for wrestling, shows the various accompaniments to this exercise. From right to left: a wrestler does *malish*, or the anointing of the body with oil; another is busy with *dand*, or push-ups; while two men wrestle with each other. The one above practises on the *lezim*, a muscle-building bow that was also used by the Maratha dancers. The last man manipulates *mogris*, or skittle-like hollow weights that were often made heavier by filling them with sand.

Kushti, or wrestling, was a common mode of keeping fit. India has one of the oldest traditions of wrestling. It is generally accepted that the sport travelled to Greece from India, and was subsequently included in the Olympics. Unlike Western wrestling, the Indian form has a religious connotation and is dedicated to Hanuman, the powerful monkey god. In this fresco, among the garments and turbans of the wrestlers, lies an image of Hanuman.

Fresco from a room of the Ram Gopal Goenka haveli in Fatehpur. Built around 1880. 53 × 73 cm.

35 In this free-hand drawing of wrestlers the artist has not used a stencil. Over the years the *pentimenti* has surfaced through the layers of lime plaster.

Detail from the Kedar Mal Ladia haveli in Mandawa. Built in 1906. 45 × 40 cm.

36 A local acrobatic show, called *nat*, which is a modest version of a roving circus. Often performed by a single family through improvised props, the show draws a spontaneous audience. While both men and women perform in the show, it is interesting to see the segregation of the sexes among the viewing public.

Fresco on the façade of the Dwarka Prasad Newatia haveli in Fatehpur. Built around 1860. 100 × 225 cm.

37 The chief architectural feature of the *haveli* was that it always faced inward, on to two
or more courtyards. While the painted façade and sides may have been impressive in
size, their tiny windows were designed to enclose the life of a *haveli*.

'Since the exteriors of the *havelis* are designed for controlled light and privacy, the
internal courtyards are all the more useful for providing good ventilation and adequate
light. Protected from strong winds and direct sun, these courts are comfortable spaces
receiving their own share of the skies and stars. As the air in the courtyard gets warmer
and lighter, it rises to make room for the fresh breeze to move through the carved
screens to take its place. This movement of air currents helps to create a micro-climate
in this structural unit, making the indoor conditions congenial to its inmates,' writes
Satish Davar.

The courtyard here, painted only in floral and geometrical designs, maintains a
symmetry of arches above the doors and windows.

Courtyard of the Mangal Chand Dalmia haveli in Chirawa. Built around 1900.

66

38 A proud Rajput combs his beard, while a servant holds a mirror for his master to admire himself. This fresco, painted in an arch above a window, is from a series painted around a courtyard. Each subject is different and shows the Shekhavati artists' ingenuity in the use of available space. Round ventilators become tables; windows become perches for birds; doors become obstacles for horses to jump over.

Details of a fresco on the Kanehram Narsingh Das Tibdiwala haveli in Jhunjhunu. Built in 1883. 130 × 80 cm.

39 A man of position riding in an *ekka*, or a hackney carriage. The driver before him waves a *chamvar*, a whisk usually made from horsehair. Society men were often shown smelling a flower. In the desert where flowers were rather uncommon, it worked purely as a pictorial symbol of status. This tradition had its precedence in Persian and Indian miniature painting and became very popular in the reign of the Mughal emperor Jahangir (1605–27).

The axle of the *ekka's* wheel is clearly off-centre, showing that much of the larger fresco drawings were done freehand, directly on to the wall surface.

Detail of a fresco on the Bhola Ram Kakraniya haveli in Chirawa. Built around 1920.
140 × 90 cm.

40 A Rajput combing and parting his beard. He is wearing the Shekhavat turban, which is tied low on one side and high on the other, exposing a lock of hair. (The turban of the Marwaris is narrower but longer.) *Pagri badal bhai* or 'brothers by exchange of turbans' was once a symbol of fraternal adoption among Rajput or a way of proving a devotion to a cause. The Rajputs also took great care of their upturned moustaches, which they considered their pride. To touch a Rajput's moustache was to invite trouble.

Detail of a fresco from the Sagar Mal Ladia haveli in Mandawa. Built around 1870.
60 × 30 cm.

68

41 A landscape with exotic trees shows Englishmen hunting in the mountains while others cycle on the tiled roads. Below them a train passes through a tunnel as guards on both sides wave flags. Although the perspective and the subject are closer to the Company School of painting, the presence of the sun and moon together recall Rajasthani miniatures.

Fresco from the Madan Lal Ranchor Lal Ladia haveli in Mandawa. Built around 1890. 200 × 300 cm.

43 Although ladies were normally expected to stay indoors in the *zenana* and to wear a veil, Rajasthan's history is not without examples of heroic women. Many went out to battle instead of taking to the fire as was customary for them after their husband's death.

This fresco may depict either Ajay Bai, the wife of Rana Sanga of Mewar who ruled from Ranthambhor to Agra, or a Bhilani. The Bhils are tribes who hunt, wander and live off the land. In Rajasthan they are also called Banwarias – professional nomadic hunting people who can hypnotize peacocks with sounds. They keep greyhounds for hunting big game.

Fresco from a room of the Motilal Sigtia haveli in Bissau. Built in 1875. 70 × 55 cm.

42 A detail from Shardul Singh's army shows the charge of the infantry. At the bottom (left) is the triangular flag of Shekhavati, with Hanuman at its centre. To the beating of drums, this flag, called *nishan* in Rajasthani, led the men in battle.

The soldiers carry swords, shields with bosses, and matchlocks, some of which are wrapped in their covers and carried on the back. In their hands is flint for their guns. Strapped to their waists are gunpowder boxes and *katars*, weapons of Indian origin used for hand-to-hand combat. The turbans show a mixture of Rajput-Mughal influence. Around their necks the soldiers wear *rudraksha* necklaces considered holy by Hindus. On their feet they wear *mochris*, named after the *mochi*, cobbler, who makes them.

In later years, the Shekhavats fought for the royal house of Amber, in many campaigns for the Mughals, and during the World Wars for the British. Their clan-mentality prompted Colonel Hendley to call Shekhavati the 'Scotland of Rajasthan'.

Detail from Shardul Singh's cremation chhatri in Parasrampura. Built in 1750.

44 Emulating the exuberance of the monarchs who planned imposing cenotaphs for themselves, the merchants of Shekhavati built ornate *chhatris* whose lime surfaces were elaborately painted. These *chhatris* were not tombs, as the Hindus are cremated, not buried.

The interior of the dome of this cremation memorial, which measures 4.5 metres in diameter, depicts the complete *Ramayana* (detail on facing plate).

Ram Gopal Poddar's chhatri in Ramgarh. Built in 1872.

45 The *Ramayana* tells the story of Rama (the seventh incarnation of Vishnu, the preserver) whose wife Sita was kidnapped by Ravana, the King of Sri Lanka. After a dramatic battle, Rama was able to rescue his wife and bring her back to Ayodhya. In this detail, he is welcomed to his city with all the royal festivities. His *guru*, Vishvamitra, applies *raj tilak* on his forehead proclaiming him king. The excellent condition of this fresco which was painted in the early 1870s can be attributed to the lack of exposure to the elements.

From a study of the style it is very likely that the artists were hired from Jaipur.

Detail from the Ramayana fresco in Ram Gopal Poddar's cremation chhatri in Ramgarh. Built in 1872. 120 × 170 cm.

46

A typical Shekhavati well, with four minarets. These were usually covered with *arayish*, a polished lime finish, or simply painted white to announce the presence of water in a way that could be seen from a distance. One of the domes of the three *chhatris* of this Seksaria well in Chirawa has an elaborately painted ceiling. The word *chhatri*, literally umbrella, is an architectural term that applies not only to the little domed pavilions built to commemorate the cremation site of an important person, but also to decorative pillared kiosks built near wells, or in palaces and gardens as an airy shelter against sun and rain.

48 The writing on the fresco reads 'Ravana'. The demon-king of Sri Lanka, Ravana had acquired great powers from the gods through his prayers and austerities. His wisdom and strength are represented by ten human heads; but his vanity, which threatened the gods themselves, and his lust, which led him to kidnap Sita, the wife of Rama, are represented by a donkey head above.

Since the gods could not take back the boons given to him, Vishnu the Preserver planned his destruction by incarnating himself as man, taking the form of Rama. It was Rama's arrow, infused with the energy of Brahma, that finally pierced Ravana's heart – a part that he had not cared to strengthen with his penances.

Detail from the frescoes in the chhatri of the Poddar well at Chirawa. Built around 1820. 20 × 35 cm.

47 The painted ceiling of this *chhatri* depicts the wedding of Rama with Sita in Mithila. The circular procession shows the gods on their celestial chariots, kings and distinguished guests which include Ganesha the elephant god drawn by two mice, Surya the Sun God on a carriage pulled by seven white horses, Indra the God of Rain mounted on his three-trunked elephant, Shiva on his Nandi bull, and a host of others. The bullock-carts, palanquins, horse-carriages, ornamented camels and elephants are a good indication of the modes of transport. The wedding ceremony is being performed around a holy fire. The ladies watch discreetly from the balconies and the terrace.

The early date of these frescoes can be attributed to the fact that wells often preceded villages and towns by several years.

Frescoes in the chhatri of the Seksaria well at Chirawa. Built around 1825. The diameter of the dome measures 270 cm.

50 A small painted structure built by the side of a well, probably as a place for resting. Floral and geometrical designs decorate the outside walls *(see detail)*. The Muslim tradition does not allow the drawing of images, permitting only floral designs, geometrical patterns and calligraphy.

Some Rajputs in Shekhavati converted to Islam in the reign of Feroze Shah Tughlak after 1351. Descendants of these Kayamkhani nawabs and the Sunni Pathans, who were dissatisfied in Maharashtra and migrated to Shekhavati, carried Muslim influence into the frescoes.

Octagonal structure by the well of Bahadur Mal Seth in Alsisar. Built around 1870.

49 Most villages and towns in Shekhavati have a *johra*, or reservoir, where rainwater gathers. This is a square or rectangular structure sometimes ornamented with arches and domes. A flight of steps on every side leads down to the water. Similar structures, called *baoris*, or step wells, are also built around natural springs.

Since Shekhavati is a semi-arid region bordering the great Thar desert of Rajasthan, water is glorified and its presence announced by monuments. The wells are adorned with minarets and *chhatris*, which often carry elaborate frescoes.

Painted arch of a chhatri of the Fateh Sagar johra in Baggar constructed in 1877.

51 Brahma, the Creator, is part of the Hindu Trinity of which Vishnu is the Preserver and Shiva the Destroyer. Strangely enough the Creator is the least worshipped of the trio of deities.

   Here the three-headed Brahma sits on a throne in his court attended by kings and holy men.

Detail from a fresco panel in a temple built in Khetri by Thakur Hari Singh of Niradhunu. Dated around 1880. 30 × 90 cm.

52 A view of what is perhaps the most exquisitely painted room in Shekhavati. This was once a jeweller's showroom, where delicately gilded frescoes added lustre to the gold and silver wares. Only the first floor of this *haveli* was used for living. Narrow stairs lead down to a strongroom, which provided the best security in the absence of metal safes and bank lockers.

Interior of the Sej Ram Podar Soné Chandi ki haveli in Mahansar. Built in 1846.

53 & 55 Surya, the Sun God, rides his chariot with seven steeds. Surya is the most important of the *navagrahas*, or nine planets, each of which is personified in Hindu mythology.

Surya's charioteer is the legless Aruna who is often shown with his wives Usha, meaning dawn, and Pratyusha, twilight.

Plate 55 shows Chandra, the Moon God, whose chariot is drawn by a deer. Two deities, Rahu, the cause of the eclipses, and Ketu, the comet, are associated with the nodes of the moon.

Frescoes from the interior of the Gopinath-ji temple in Malsisar. Built in 1840 by Kanwar Tarvat Singh of Malsisar. 15 × 20 cm each.

54 An intricately worked and painted verandah from the temple of *Shani*, the Saturday God. Besides the floral motifs, mirror-work, and mythological scenes, the work on the floor is particularly interesting. This process is called *arayish* (or *pana* in Shekhavati), and involves a coating of fine marble powder and ground shell mixed with lime. Before it sets, it can be inlaid with glass, mirror and stone to form colourful patterns.

While the large mirrors were imported, the small convex mirrors for the mosaic were locally produced from thin glass polished with mercury. These small mirrors were seldom transported; it was more common to invite the mirror-man to the site of construction.

Painted interior of the Sanichar-ji Shani temple in Ramgarh. Built around 1824.

56 A detail of a Shivaite saint with his *trishul*, or trident, looped
earrings, leopardskin, and symbolic third eye. Shiva, the third
member of the Hindu Trinity, occupies the role of Destroyer of the
Universe at the end of each phase of the cosmic cycle, and is known
to have a bad temper. The bloodshot eyes of the saint in this fresco
are probably a representation of this anger. Many of Shiva's
followers are *yogis*, since Shiva himself is often depicted as a yogic
recluse living on Mount Kailasa. Shivaites also wear snakes around
their necks or arms, rub ash on their bodies, and remain semi-
naked.

*Detail from a frescoed room of the Sukhdev Das Ganeriwala (now
Kanoria) haveli in Mukundgarh. Built in 1880. 25 × 40 cm.*

57 Shiva, the God of Destruction, has come to be, in Dr T. S. Maxwell's
words: 'a god of paradoxes: withdrawn ascetic/universal
progenitor; the male principle/man and woman in one; wild
huntsman of the forest/teacher of the arts and sciences in the
mountains; creator/destroyer; naked wanderer in the wilderness
carrying a skull, frightener of men and women/the supreme dancer
who leads men to salvation. All these oppositions are resolved and
accounted for in his mythology.'

In this fresco the river Ganges flows out from Shiva's matted
hair. The god wears a necklace of skulls and is adorned by serpents
who, along with the bull Nandi, are his symbols.

Fresco from the fort of Surajgarh. Built in 1799. 40 × 30 cm.

58 & 59

Ganesha, the son of Shiva and Parvati, is the elephant-headed guardian of the portal. He is always present at the entrance of a *haveli*, and is seen here in an over-ornate gateway. Accompanying the god are his two wives Riddhi and Siddhi, the artist's imagination having multiplied them to four. Normally Ganesha is shown seated on a mouse, who is his carrier. Legend has it that when all the gods arrived to attend the wedding of Krishna with Rukmini, Ganesha was asked to stay back since his vehicle was too small. Annoyed at this decision, Ganesha ordered an army of mice to dig up the road, causing the divine chariots and vehicles to stick in the soft earth. When an invitation finally came, Ganesha is supposed to have told Krishna: 'I shall marry first, then you will; I shall have two wives, you will have only one; and those who pray, shall always worship me before you.' These conditions were accepted by the gods before proceeding to the wedding.

The angels with trumpets are *gandharas*, celestial-beings often represented as flying musicians. More common in Indian mythology are *apsaras*, the beautiful nymphs who are the courtesans of the gods but who sometimes descend on earth to seduce men.

Entrance of the Jankidas Ramgopal Kajaria haveli in Kajara. Built in 1912.

60 Krishna appears three times in the *rasa mandala*, or the joyful circular dance, performed here with three *gopis*, or milkmaids. Above, he plays the flute for Radha, his favourite *gopi*, while her friends wave fly-whisks.

On both sides, cows attended by *gopis* adore Krishna, who is also the protector of cattle. The fresco seems to borrow its imagery from *pichhwais*, the painted temple cloths hung as a backdrop to the idols of Krishna in Nathadwara.

Frescoes around the windows of the Ishwar Das Ram Narain Poddar haveli in Fatehpur. Built around 1890.

61 Krishna, the blue-faced one, shown in a popular scene, *vastra harana*. Krishna has stolen the clothes of the *gopis* who were bathing in the Jamuna river and climbed a *kadamba* tree. They plead with him to return their garments; he smiles and plays his flute. Crocodiles seem to look on in amusement, and a parrot turns its head to watch the fun.

Among the milkmaids, Krishna's favourite was Radha, said to be the wife of a cowherd named Ayana. But Radha's love for Krishna is elevated above lust, and treated as allegorical of the soul's longing for God.

Krishna, the eighth incarnation of Vishnu, is the ideal child, the ideal lover, the ideal soldier and philosopher. It is interesting to note that on the plains of the Kurukshetra, the same amorous and mischievous Krishna became Arjuna's charioteer, declaiming the wisdom that gave birth to the *Bhagavad Gita*.

Frescoes around a window of the Pansari haveli in Sri Madhopur. Built around 1890.

62 Eight entangled *gopis* contort to form an elephant for Krishna. Such compositions are called *navakunjara* and are variations of the *rasa lila* theme, often used by artists to show their drawing skill. Sometimes, similar scenes were depicted in erotic paintings where amorous couples formed palaces, swings or animals.

The long hair of Krishna curling on the neck is called *girda*, and is typical of the Jaipur School of painting under Maharaja Sawai Ram Singh (1834–80).

Fresco in a room of the Ram Gopal Goenka haveli in Fatehpur. Built around 1850.
60 × 40 cm.

63 The fresco that borders the mirror-work ceiling depicts a square version of the *rasa mandala*. The pointed skirts show the influence of the Jodhpur School. Krishna, playing his flute, called the *gopis* of Vrindavan to admire the full moon. They found his flute irresistible – which has its metaphoric connotations – and were lured into dancing with him. He willingly multiplied himself to be with each of them.

It was this manifestation of Krishna as Gopinath-ji, the Lord of the Milkmaids, that was worshipped by Mokul, the father of Rao Shekha. Even today, Gopinath-ji is the patron deity of the Shekhavats.

Fresco on the entrance ceiling of the Nand Lal Devra haveli in Fatehpur. Built around 1860.
300 × 300 cm.

64 Krishna lifting Mount Govardhana to protect the herders and their cows from the rain. The caption below the mountain reads: *'Nakh par girvar dharo'* ('Holding the mountain by the fingernail'). To the right of Krishna are Nanda and Yashoda, his foster-parents. His real parents, Vasudev and Devaki, had to abandon him for fear of his being killed by the wicked King Kamsa. Indra, the most powerful Vedic god – who was both war god and weather god – was in the later mythology of the Puranas lowered to a secondary divinity and a rival of Krishna. Here Indra kneels near Krishna's feet asking forgiveness for causing the rain. This image of Krishna as Govardhananath is worshipped as Shri Nath-ji.

The curling clouds above are typical of the Jodhpur style of painting and are here personified as human. The blue is still the natural blue from indigo. It was after 1890 that synthetic blue from Germany began to replace the indigenous natural colour.

Detail from a fresco panel in a temple built in Khetri by Thakur Hari Singh of Niradhunu. Dated around 1880. 30 × 90 cm.

65 A legend from the *Mahabharata* shows Bhima, the strongest of the five Pandava brothers, shaking a tree where his hundred cousins, the Kauravas, were playing. The cousins fall like ripe fruit, while birds take to their wings. Bhima the Terrible was the second of the Pandavas and son of Vayu, God of the Wind.

This fresco, painted just outside the Shekhavati area, represents the earliest tradition of frescoes in Rajasthan. The structure on which this fresco is painted, attributed to the late Akbar period (around 1600), is supposed to have been the site of a royal hunt. On the basis of the turbans and dresses painted, some scholars assign this to the early Jahangir period (around 1610).

There are remnants of frescoes on one of the walls of the Mughal palaces in Fatehpur Sikri (near Agra), roughly of the same period. Since these are painted only on the interior of the room of a Rajput princess, they indicate that this was an indigenous tradition rather than one borrowed from the Mughals; otherwise they would have made a more lavish use of this technique.

Detail from a painted kiosk at the Bairat (Viratnagar) garden retreat on the Alwar to Jaipur road. Dated between 1585 and 1615.

66 A scene from the *Ramayana*. Rama, King of Ayodhya, was forced to expel his wife Sita from his kingdom in order to appease his subjects, who believed she had been unfaithful to him. She retreated to the forest and there gave birth to twins, Lav and Kush. Sita later proved her purity by walking through fire, and Rama admitted his folly and took her back.

Here Sita is seen with Guru Valmiki, the author of the original *Ramayana*, and her twins.

Kush was to become the founder of the proud Kachhawaha clan which traces its ancestry to the sun and from which the Shekhavats also draw their lineage. Lav's descendants are called Badgoojars.

Fresco from the Nandlal Bagaria haveli in Chirawa. Built in 1917. 180 × 95 cm.

बालम्किजीलोकसःसीताजी

67 Hanuman, the powerful monkey-god of the *Ramayana* who symbolizes the ideal servant, is seen here with ten arms. The eight extra arms can be ascribed to the imagination of the folk artists who often shaped their gods after their own fancy.

   Among the other services that he performed for his master Rama, Hanuman uprooted and carried a mountain on which grew the *Sanjivani buti*, a special herb required to cure Lakshmana, the younger brother of Rama. The mountain in this fresco shows houses and trees, and Hanuman is seen crushing Lankini *sursa*, a demoness who obstructed his way. Hanuman also organized, with his army of monkeys, the building of a bridge from India to Ceylon (Sri Lanka). This enabled Rama's army to cross over and rescue Sita from Ravana, the ten-headed ruler of Lanka. After Sita was rescued, Hanuman set light to his tail and waved it throughout Ravana's kingdom, setting it aflame.

   Hanuman was born of the wind, and is widely worshipped throughout India; his faithfulness and self-surrender have become proverbial.

Fresco from the interior of the Gopinath-ji temple in Malsisar. Built in 1840 by Kanwar Tarvat Singh of Malsisar. 20 × 20 cm.

68 Another version of Hanuman as he flies with the mountain on his palm. In the other hand he holds a *gada*, a round mace that only the super-strong could wield. Before the fresco is a pillar-like container for growing the *tulsi*, or holy basil, a plant sacred to the Hindus. The medicinal properties of the *tulsi* are legion; it is known to purify both the atmosphere and the body. Traditional Hindu homes still grow it on their thresholds and devout housewives worship it as an embodiment of all divinity.

Fresco in the courtyard of Gopal-ji's temple attached to the Shiv Narayan Birla haveli in Pilani. This temple was built on the site of an earlier temple estimated to be three hundred years old. The fresco here dates from 1907. 300 × 230 cm.

69 An early fresco painted only in organic colours shows a Rajput couple embracing. While the masculinity of a Rajput male is proverbial, women were expected to combine their feminine graces with hearts of steel.

The lady in the fresco holds a wine jug and could perhaps be a courtesan. Opium, liquor and other intoxicants were very common and became the cause of the decline of many a Rajput family. James Tod, writing in the early nineteenth century, also tells us of the 'sale of aphrodisiacs, which are sought after with great avidity'.

Fresco from a ceiling in the Mandawa Fort. Built in 1760. 30 × 20 cm.

70 What may to others be an everyday scene of lovers exchanging a kiss was almost scandalous for the traditional Rajasthanis. In this rather unusual example, the artists has merged the profiles to create an interesting effect.

Fresco on the Jhabarmal Seth haveli in Alsisar. Built around 1900. 80 × 60 cm.

94

71 One of a series of *trompe l'oeil* frames painted along the border of a ceiling. While the painting of erotic pictures on paper was common, examples of erotic frescoes are few, presumably because they could not be put away or concealed. These must have been executed only when specially commissioned by an interested patron. Philip Rawson tells us of a bygone era when the moral standards were less constricting: 'Great classics of erotic technique have been composed in India – *Kama Sutra, Kokashastra, Ratirahasya,* etc. Every activity and technique they describe has its own special pleasure; and they teach pleasure as a goal both socially acceptable and personally desirable'.

Fresco in a room of the Shiv Narain Nemani haveli in Churi Ajitgarh. Built in 1918. 37 × 65 cm.

72 Three erotic scenes secreted in the doorway of an inner room, probably a bedroom. It is interesting to note the discretion with which such matters were treated. Normally, during the day, when the doors remained open, only Krishna and Radha's religious tableau (to the left) was visible. It was only in the privacy provided by a closed door that these erotic paintings could be appreciated.

Frescoes in a room in the Sukhdev Das Ganeriwala haveli in Mukundgarh, now belonging to the Kanorias. Dated around 1880.

73 Lithography, invented by an Austrian in 1798, came to India with the British in the 1820s, according to Jaya Appasamy. At first it was used purely for functional purposes, such as survey charts and maps, which were almost always in black and white; but gradually, during the 1850s and 1860s, its use spread to portraiture, book illustration, sacred subjects and decorative arts. Here, in a well-preserved room inside the Singhania *haveli* in Fatehpur, English lithographs hang just as they did in the heyday of the *havelis*. These curious lithographs, often adorned with gold paper appliqué, were commonly imported into India by the well-to-do. They became convenient models for artists who wanted to keep up with the changing tastes of their patrons.

An interior of the Jagannath Singhania haveli in Fatehpur. Built in 1870.

74 Frescoes on the exterior of the Chodhari *haveli*, in a street adjoining the Singhania *haveli*, show how the lithographs were adapted to the fresco treatment. The Indian artists have somewhat exaggerated the postures of the English ladies, who play coquettishly with their fans and pearls, while exposing bare shoulders and plunging necklines.

Western lithographs did more than influence the fresco painters. As Jaya Appasamy points out, 'the process of lithography itself was adopted by Indian artists for the creation of popular pictures, the forerunners of the ubiquitous calendar picture which is a principal kind of mass oriented art even today.'

The Rameshwarlal Chodhari haveli in Fatehpur. Built around 1870. Each frieze measures 60 × 100 cm.

75 A Dhola-Maru scene on the façade of the Behari Lal Chamaria *haveli* in Ratan Nagar.
Built around 1880. (For legend, see Plate 17.)

76 The foliated arch of a gateway shows a painted *haveli* across the street. The panel at the bottom depicts an army camp. To the left are musicians and soldiers, and to the right, camels, bullocks and horses carry cannons and cannon-balls. Other painted tableaux adorn the areas between the stone brackets. The rooms on the first floor with carved wooden windows project over the street, their stone railings worked in relief. Pigeons huddle and coo in their shade.
Façade of the Ramji Lal Kedia haveli in Lachhmangarh. Built around 1880. The painted panel below is 40 × 600 cm.

77 A parade of Red Coats with musicians leading the infantry. This seems to be a peace-time version, since the soldiers carry a gun in one hand and a flower in the other. After the Sepoy Mutiny of 1857, the British reorganized their troops, increasing the ratio: one British soldier to every seven Indians. For well over a century and a half the British army made India its second home. The famous remark, usually attributed to Lady Curzon, that 'the two ugliest things in India are a water-buffalo and a British soldier,' did not seem to apply to Rajasthan, which saw much less of the British army than many other areas. Soldiers from the northern races proved themselves superior to the southerners. It gradually became British policy to recruit more from the north. Among these, the Rajputs ranked highly, along with the Sikhs.
Fresco on the Devkaran Ram Kumar Chokhani haveli in Nawalgarh. Built around 1820. 70 × 230 cm.

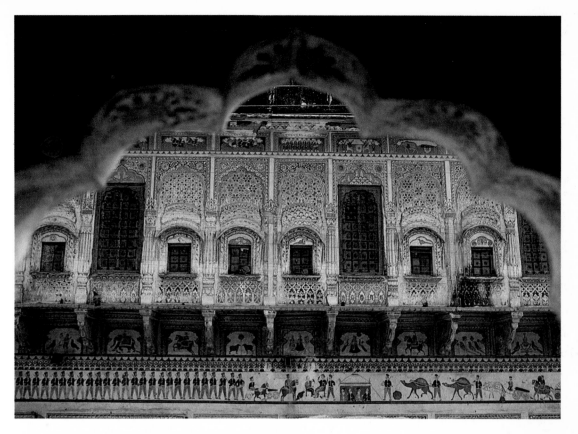

78 While turquoise and lapis lazuli were crushed and powdered in the royal ateliers to make blue pigments for miniature paintings, for frescoes, which were larger, indigo seemed more economical. It was after 1890 that synthetic blue from Germany arrived to replace the more inconvenient natural pigment. The *haveli* here, painted only in blue, boasts its modernity by its use of the new imported colour. The whole effect is much like the blue and white porcelain from China.

Windows overlooking the courtyard of the Gauri Lal Biyani haveli in Sikar. Built in 1920.

79 An English couple with hats and umbrellas riding in a buggy. Their stiff postures typify the protocol, formality and conformity that ruled the lives of the British officers in India.

The oval wheels and the connecting chains show the artist's clumsy notion of the working of carriages – or, at best, his lack of attention to technical details.

It is popularly believed that Seth Duli Chand of Chirawa rode a carriage with six horses. Since the British government allowed only two horses on the carriages of commoners (rajas were permitted four-horse carriages), the Seth had to pay a fine each time he took his carriage out.

Fresco on the Manohar Lal Vaid haveli in Chirawa. Built in 1929. 80 × 120 cm.

80 A Rajasthani rides a bicycle, its inspiration surely coming either from the circus or from a false understanding of the penny-farthing. Oddly enough, the round cap of the rider is not sporting headgear, since it was normally worn by the mercantile community. The *dhoti* around his legs does not seem to be an ideal dress for pedalling.

Fresco on the Badridas Vaid haveli in Lachhmangarh. Built around 1890. 100 × 60 cm.

81 The bicycle was not suitable desert transport and it seems very unlikely that the inhabitants of Rajasthan had ever seen one at this time. However, during the Company Period (1760–1880), lithographs and oleographs from Europe brought Western inventions to India. The safety bicycle, close to the design we know today, had become popular in Europe in 1885.

The fresco here shows a 'Feringhee' (foreigner) riding one of these early bicycles. His *topi* is probably an artist's version of the Cawnpore Tent Club helmet which remained in fashion in British India for over half a century. The trousers are tied with *pattis*, or straps, to keep them from catching in the chain.

The panel above shows a ship – a sight which seems rather stranded in the desert.

Fresco from the Madan Lal Ranchor Lal Ladia haveli in Mandawa. Built around 1890. 90 × 90 cm.

उड़नेवाला जहाज

83 The foremost room of a temple that opened on to the main street is now a shop. Framed oleographs of gods and heroes sell alongside imitation Coca-Cola bottles in plastic, ball-point pens, biscuits, footwear and clothing. At home, beside these popular oleographs of the gods, the villagers often hang portraits of Gandhi and Nehru. Over the years figures from history ascend to a semi-deified position.

Pupul Jayakar writes: 'Rural India today is in a state of flux. It finds itself challenged at all levels of life, ritual, art and function. Exploding populations, an indiscriminate destruction of environment, a continuing revolution in communications, and the accelerated penetration of the technology and artefacts of urban industrial societies into interior isolated villages have generated enormous pressures and brought into the rural situation new challenges and tensions. Everywhere we turn we see the whisper of the new technological culture – bullock carts with rubber tyres, transistors in village squares, mass produced Krishna sculptures in painted plaster sold at village fairs.'

The left façade of Madan Mohan-ji's temple in Sikar. Built in 1920.

82 When the Wright brothers assembled their first aeroplane in 1903, using their bicycle factory as a laboratory, the West saw bright prospects for quicker travel. In India, the news at that time can have occasioned only a flight of fancy. The caption below the fresco of the Wright brothers and their plane reads 'udnewala jahaz', 'the flying ship'.

Fresco on the Mohan Lal Newatia haveli in Mandawa. Built in the late 1930s.

84 Lord Curzon's Great Durbar of 1903, a remarkable demonstration of an imperial power at its zenith, was enough to tyrannize the traditions of the 'natives'. All the rajas and businessmen who were invited to watch the spectacle must have thought it a matter of great pride to be associated with it.

In Shekhavati, an era of emulating the British had already begun before the turn of the century. The façade of this early twentieth-century *haveli* in Chirawa depicts several European scenes: a couple strolling with their dogs, a buggy, a gentleman with a gun, a victoria carriage. The blue pillars, the *trompe l'oeil* blinds, the theatrical red curtains and the glass lanterns have already disowned the Indian traditions.

In Chirawa were reputed to have lived the kind of multi-millionaire Marwaris who wore a dress for one occasion only; before a second wearing it was sent to be dry-cleaned abroad. Another such *seth* is reported to have served tea to a British officer, the water for which was boiled by burning the newly released paper currency!

Façade of the Keshav Dev Dalmia haveli in Chirawa. Built in 1909.

85 In 1803, the Princes of Rajputana entered into a treaty with the British government which was ratified in 1818. This brought in a British Resident who conducted local affairs. By 1860, the British had a strong foothold, and the Indians began to imitate their taste. It became increasingly popular to dress in an English way and to cultivate the English language and mannerisms.

The content of the Shekhavati frescoes changed from the Rajput, Mughal and folk themes to Western subjects such as trains, cars, bicycles, carriages, and European portraits. Regular appearances are made by Queen Victoria, King George V, Queen Mary and even Jesus Christ.

A superficial understanding of some of the products of technology resulted in lopsided trains, imaginary cars, and bicycles that could almost certainly not be pedalled.

The car on this fresco in Churu seems to have been inspired by one of the Rolls Royces of the Maharaja of Bikaner. Churu, once part of Shekhavati, was annexed by Bikaner in 1512.

Fresco on the Hazari Mal Sardar Mal Madan Chand Kothari haveli in Churu. Built around 1915. 60 × 100 cm.

86 & 87

The laying of railway tracks in the 1850s began the task of making India look more like a country than a continent. Although the first train reached Shekhavati only in 1916, vivid descriptions had arrived long before.

Providing a convenient linear pattern, the train soon became one of the favourite motifs of the fresco painter. But his understanding of the working of a locomotive was far from sound, and the rural interpretation came closer to a child's drawing than a reproduction of reality.

Both trains here show the imagination of the artists who painted them. The lower fresco also depicts the older modes of transport – horses, camels and carriages – which were naturally more familiar to the mural painter. They are interspersed with flowing trees reminiscent of Jain miniatures of the fifteenth century.

ABOVE: *Fresco of a train on the haveli or Ramgopal Poddar in Ramgarh. Built around 1865. 40 × 100 cm.*

BOTTOM: *Fresco of a train on the Shiv Narain Mahadev Prasad Patwari haveli in Nim Ka Thana. Built in 1899. 160 × 200 cm.*

88 At most ceremonial functions in British India a band was a common sight. Many of the Civil Lines built by the British had a Company Bagh, or public garden, with a bandstand. Here a blond English bandmaster is seen conducting his band, a baton in one hand, a hat and a cigar in the other. The chain of his pocket watch shows prominently.

This is the *vilayati baja*, or English band. The indigenous type is the *Arabi baja*, a band which came to India with the Muslims and is normally heard during the Muharram festival.

Fresco from the Chhatra Bhuj Dalmia haveli in Chirawa (now whitewashed). Built around 1890. 75 × 110 cm.

89 In the early days, Englishwomen in India 'faced months of boredom and loneliness while their husbands were away on active service, years when their children were away growing up into strangers,' writes Charles Allen. They filled long hours of leisure with housekeeping, sewing, supervising the gardens and maintaining a retinue of servants. This fresco on a *haveli* of the early twentieth century shows an English lady listening to a gramophone.

Allen observes the changes that came about in the later years: 'after The Great War, . . . memsahibs came off their pedestals and took it upon themselves to move into Indian society, taking more active roles in the welfare of their household staff or the men under their husbands' command, giving purdah parties for their Indian opposite numbers, even taking up nursing, scouting or other forms of voluntary work'.

Since exposure to the British life was limited, lithographs and photographs provided a ready reference. To these, the artist often made his own imaginative additions influenced by the popular work of Raja Ravi Verma of Travancore.

Fresco from the Balmukand Bansidhar Rathi haveli in Lachhmangarh. Built in 1910. 130 × 65 cm.

90 Two tailors at work: one takes the measurements of a customer while the other changes the sewing thread. Hybrid fashions resulting from the interaction between the Indian and the British cultures were almost instantly accepted among the Indians because they signified an association with the rulers. Here, bordered coats are worn with the traditional *dhoti*. The elegant dining-chair with a pair of scissors seems an afterthought of the artist, perhaps added to fill the gap between the men. However, the perspective is wrong and one leg of the chair overlaps the tailor's leg.

Fresco on the haveli of Ram Kumar Shri Niwas Jangid in Nawalgarh. Built in 1922. 90 × 160 cm.

91 A *haveli* adapted to modern times. The room below now serves as a tailor's shop, while the frescoed arches have been whitewashed and painted with an election slogan demanding the 'precious vote' of the electorate. Of the windows above, three are painted in *trompe l'oeil* to maintain the symmetry of the façade. Wealthy *seths* and their wives, dressed in formal attire, look out on to the street.

The left façade of the Hanuman Bux Ram Kumar Dangayach haveli in Nawalgarh. Built in 1884.

92 Europeans courting on a bench in the park. In a society where women were kept in *purdah* and rarely allowed to meet any men, a couple flirting in a public place must have been a fascinating sight. The lady's parasol and mink boa, the gentleman's cigarette and posture, show the artist's particular interests. The modelling of the figures and the manner in which the rocks, waves and the trees are shaded differ greatly from the Indian tradition.

The declaration of English as the official language in March 1835 had far-reaching effects. A new world of intellectual, moral and spiritual values was opened to the Indians, and helped to bridge some of the gaps between the two cultures.

Fresco on the Prem Sukhdas Chhawchharia haveli in Nawalgarh. Built in 1897, it now belongs to Mohanlal Hiralal Sarawgi. 150 × 100 cm.

93 A Rajput guards the inner entrance of a *haveli*. The frescoes, after blooming for over two hundred years, seem to have gone to seed on this over-decorated gateway.

It is not uncommon for a colonized people to turn their backs on their indigenous arts and blindly follow the tastes of their rulers. Oleographs from Europe, copied in India, had already transformed popular bazaar art. When this influence came into the frescoes and architecture, it resulted in an extravagant use of line and colour, in a different use of mirror-work, and in a fascination for imported tiles. The rooms in this *haveli* have Japanese tiles painted with Mount Fuji.

While this hybridization brought about a decline in taste, the end of the era of wall paintings was further prompted by the absence of the Marwaris themselves. As their activities widened and diversified in the cities, interest in their ancestral homes waned.

The artists, now without sponsors, migrated to other places and other professions.

The inner entrance of the Jwala Prasad Bhartia haveli in Fatehpur. Built in 1928.

Sites and chronology of wall paintings in India

Ajanta caves *(Maharashtra)*	second and first centuries BC fifth, sixth and seventh centuries AD
Bagh caves *(Dhar District, Madhya Pradesh)*	fourth to sixth centuries
Pitalkhora *(Aurangabad District, Maharashtra)*	fourth to sixth centuries
Badami rock-cut temples *(Bijapur District, Karnataka)*	sixth century
Kailasanatha temple *(Ellora, Aurangabad District, Maharashtra)*	eighth century
Sittannavasala cave temple *(Tiruchirapalli District, Tamil Nadu)*	ninth century
Alchi monastery *(near Leh, Ladakh)*	tenth and eleventh centuries
Brihedeswara temple *(Tanjore, Tamil Nadu)*	eleventh century
Hampi temples and palaces *(Bellary District, Karnataka)*	fifteenth century
Lepakshi Shiva temple *(Anantapur District, Andhra Pradesh)*	sixteenth century
Akbar's tomb, Sikandra *(near Agra, Uttar Pradesh)*	sixteenth century
Thirumalai temple *(Tamil Nadu)*	sixteenth and seventeenth centuries
Orissa maths *(mainly in Puri, Orissa)*	sixteenth to nineteenth centuries
Vadakkunathan temple *(Trichur, Kerala)*	seventeenth and eighteenth centuries
Srirangapattam *(Mysore District, Karnataka)*	eighteenth century
Mattancheri palace *(Cochin, Kerala)*	eighteenth century
Palaces of the rulers of Punjab and Himachal Pradesh in regional styles of miniature paintings	eighteenth and nineteenth centuries

Cenotaphs, forts, palaces, temples and homes of the Rajputs and Marwaris in Rajasthan	eighteenth, nineteenth and twentieth centuries

Ritual and folk paintings on mud huts:

Madhubani *(Bihar)*	living tradition
Warli *(Maharashtra)*	living tradition
Chhota Udaipur *(Gujarat)*	living tradition
Balikondalo *(Orissa)* etc.	living tradition

ala gila Rajasthani term for *fresco buono*, the technique of painting on damp lime walls.

apsara beautiful celestial nymphs who were the courtesans of gods but sometimes descended on the earth to seduce men.

arayish a process for giving a polished finish to lime floors and walls.

Arjuna one of the five Pandava brothers, the heroes of the epic *Mahabharata*. In the *Bhagwad Gita*, Krishna is Arjuna's charioteer.

avatara an incarnation of god, usually associated with the *dasavataras* of Vishnu.

Ayodhya the ancient capital from where Rama ruled.

bagh a garden.

baithak an arcaded but closed space at the entrance of a *haveli* where men met and conducted business.

Bhagavad Gita 'Song Celestial', refers to the part of the *Mahabharata* where Krishna propounds his wisdom to Arjuna.

Bhima the Terrible was the second of the five Pandava brothers.

chhatri a pillared kiosk by a well, in a garden, or erected as a cenotaph.

chillum an earthen pipe for smoking tobacco or hashish.

Diwali the festival of lights when Lakshmi the Goddess of Wealth is worshipped.

devi goddess.

dhoti nether garment worn usually by male Hindus.

durbar a royal court.

Feringhee a foreigner, though in the Orient it referred to a Portuguese.

fresco buono or 'true' fresco, the technique of painting on damp plaster.

fresco secco or tempera the technique of painting on dry plaster.

gada a war mace.

gandhara celestial musicians

Ganga a goddess who is the personification of River Ganges.

gopis the cowherd girls usually associated with Krishna and Vrindavan.

Gopinath-ji Lord of the Gopis, a manifestation of Krishna.

guru a religious teacher

Hanuman the monkey god of the *Ramayana*.

haveli a large city house.

hookah the water pipe or hubble-bubble.

Indra the war god and rain god of the Vedas.

ishta devi /devata goddess/god who is worshipped as a personal god.

Jamuna a goddess who is the personification of the River Jamuna.

jauhar the custom of group self immolation of women and children after the men had been lost in battle.

johra a water reservoir for gathering and storing rain water.

Kachhawahas a Rajput clan descended from Kush, the son of Rama.

Kauravas the hundred cousins of the Pandavas who ruled from Kurus and fought the Pandavas.

kothi a country house surrounded by a garden.

Krishna the eighth incarnation of Vishnu the Preserver.

Kshatriya the warrior class.

kula devata the patron diety of a family or clan.

Kurukshetra in present day Haryana, site of the battle of Mahabharata.

Kush one of the twins of Rama whose progeny is called Kachhawahas.

lakh a hundred thousand.

Lakshmana the brother of Rama.

Lav one of the twins of Rama whose progeny is called Badgoojars.

Mahabharata the epic poem about the civil war between the Pandavas and the Kauravas.

mahal palace.

mahout elephant driver.

mantra a magical verbal formula which is chanted in meditation and worship.

Marwari the mercantile community of Rajasthan.

memsahib a term used by a servant to address his mistress.

Mount Govardhana the holy mount which Krishna lifted to protect the villagers and their cows from the rain.

Mughal the Muslim dynasty that ruled large parts of north-western India from the early 16th to the mid-18th century.

Muharram a Muslim festival.

Narikunjara an amalgam of gopis to form an animal, a palanquin, a swing or whatever the artist fancied.

Navakunjara a fantastic creature created from a combination of animals associated with Krishna.

nawab Muslim princeling.

paan betel leaf with lime, pieces of areca nut, tobacco and other ingredients.

Pandavas five brothers, the victors in the battle of Mahabharata.

pentimento something painted over in a picture which later becomes visible again.

Puranas ancient Hindu myths and legends.

purdah curtain symbolizing the veil behind which women remained.

Radha the consort of Krishna and his favorite gopi.

Rajput 'sons of kings', the proud members of Rajasthan's warrior class.

Rajputana the medieval name of Rajasthan.

Rama hero of the Ramayana, the seventh incarnation of Vishnu.

Ramayana the epic story of Rama.

rasa lila the amorous games of Krishna.

rasa mandala the cosmic circular dance of Krishna and the gopis.

Ravana the ten-headed demon-king of Sri Lanka who abducted Sita.

sahib a European master.

sati a virtuous wife. This term also applies to widows who burnt themselves on the funeral pyres of their husbands.

seth a wealthy merchant.

Shri Nath-ji a manifestation of Krishna worshipped in Nathadwara in southern Rajasthan.

Sikh the turbaned martial race of the Punjab.

Suryavanshis Rajputs who claim descent from the sun.

tazim an anklet of honour given by a Maharaja to his vassals.

thakur a vassal of a Maharaja.

thikana a small fiefdom or state.

tibari a three-arched space at the entrance of a *haveli* where men met and conducted business.

topi a hat. The word is adopted from the Hindi.

trompe l'oeil an illusion of three dimensions used in still life painting or in plaster ornamentation.

tulsi the holy basil, a household plant, tended and worshipped by Hindu women.

Valmiki the author of the original *Ramayana*.

Vayu the vedic God of the Wind.

Vedas ancient Hindu scriptures.

Vishnu the Preserver, whose ten incarnations have restored the balance of cosmic forces of the universe.

Vrindavan a place near Mathura where Krishna is supposed to have grazed his cows.

zenana the quarter to which ladies confined themselves in a *haveli*, palace or fort.

Bibliography

AGARAWALA, R. A.: *Marwar Murals, Agam Prakashan*, New Delhi, 1977

ALLEN, CHARLES: *Raj – A Scrapbook of British India 1877–1947*, Indian Book Company & André Deutsch, New Delhi/London, 1977

ANAND, UMA: *Guide to Rajasthan*, Indian Tourism Development Corporation, New Delhi, 1975

APPASAMY, JAYA: *Early Calcutta Lithographs*, lecture, India International Centre, 1981.

– *Indian Paintings of the Company School*, lecture, India International Centre, 1980

BARRETT, DOUGLAS AND GREY, BASIL: *Indian Painting*, Albert Skira, Geneva, 1963

BROOKE, COL J. C.: *Political History of Jaipur*

BUSSABARGER, ROBERT F. & ROBINS, BETTY DASHEN: *The Everyday Art of India*, Dover Publications, New York, 1968

CAROLL, DAVID: 'The Taj Mahal – India under the Moghuls', *Newsweek*, New York, 1972

COOPER, ILAY: 'Wall Paintings in Rajasthan', article, *The Illustrated Weekly of India*, July 25, 1976. 'The Painted Houses of Shekhavati', article, New Delhi, December, 1979.

DAVAR, SATISH: article in *Marg* Vol. XXX No 4, 'Homage to Jaipur', Marg Publications, Bombay, September, 1977

DUNDLOD, HARNATH SINGH OF: *The Shekhavats and their Lands*, Rajasthan Educational Printers, Jaipur, 1970

FERGUSSON, JAMES & BURGESS, JAMES: *History of India & Eastern Architecture*, revised and edited with additions by R. Phene Spiers (2 vols), Munshiram Manoharlal, New Delhi, 1967

FRANKLIN, W.: *Military Memoirs of G. Thomas*, 1803

GASCOIGNE, BAMBER: *The Great Moghuls*, Jonathan Cape, London, 1971

GODDEN, JON & RUMER: *Shivas's Pigeons – An experience of India*, Alfred A. Knopf/Viking Press, New York, 1972

GOETZ, HERMAN: *The Art and Architecture of Bikaner State*, Government of Bikaner State and the Royal India and Pakistan Oxford Society by Bruno Cassier, 1950

GUPTA, MOHAN LAL: *Frescoes and Wall Paintings of Rajasthan*, privately published, Jaipur, 1965

HAVELL, E. B.: *Indian Architecture*, S. Chand, New Delhi, 1971

HENDLEY, T. H.: *Rulers of India and the Chiefs of Rajputana*, W. Griggs, London, 1897

HUTCHINS, FRANCIS G.: *Young Krishna*, Amarata Press, West Franklin, 1980

IVORY, JAMES: *Autobiography of a Princess*, Harper and Row, New York, 1975

JAIN, KESARLAL AJMERA & JAIN, JAWAHARLAL: *Jaipur Album or all about Jaipur*, Rajasthan Directories Publishing House, Jaipur 1935

JAYAKAR, PUPUL: *The Earthen Drum*, National Museum, New Delhi, 1981 and article in *Marg* Vol. XXXIII No. 1, Warp and Woof, Marg Publications, Bombay, December, 1979

JOSHI, O. P.: *Painted Folklore and Folklore Painters of India*, Concept Publishing Company, Delhi, 1976

KAPUR, GEETA: *Contemporary Indian Artists*, Vikas Publishing House, New Delhi, 1978

KAUL, H. K.: *Travellers' India – An Anthology* (ed.), Oxford University Press, Delhi, 1979

KHANDALAVALA, KARL: *Wall Paintings from Amber*, Lalit Kala Akademi, New Delhi, 1977

MADURO, RONALDO: *Artistic Creativity in a Brahmin Painter Community* (thesis), Berkeley University, 1973

MANDAWA, DEVI SINGH OF: *Shardul Singh-ji Shekhavat* (Hindi), Shardul Education Trust, Jhunjhunu, 1970

MAXWELL, DR T. S.: 'Mythology of Shiva and the Goddess' (from the catalogue of *In the Image of Man* exhibition, London) Arts Council of Great Britain, 1982

MEHTA, RAMA: *Inside the Haveli*, Arnold/Heinemann, New Delhi, 1977

MEHTA, RUSTAM J.: *Handicrafts and Industrial Arts of India*, Taraporevala, Bombay, 1960

RAWSON, PHILIP: *Erotic Art of India*, Thames and Hudson, London, 1978

– *The Indian Cult of Ecstasy: Tantra*, Thames and Hudson, London, 1973

SHARMA, JHABARMAL: *Khetri Ka Itihas* (Hindi) and *Sikar Ka Itihas* (Hindi), 1922, Rajasthan Agencies, Calcutta, 1927

SHERRING, M. A.: *The Tribes and Castes of Rajasthan*, London, 1881

SKELTON, ROBERT: *Rajasthani Temple Hangings of the Krishna Cult*, The American Federation of Arts, 1973

SRIVASTAVA, SATYA PRAKASH: 'Wall Paintings – technique of their execution and preservation', *Journal of Indian Museums*

TAVERNIER, J. B.: *Travels in India* . . . translated by V. Ball, edited by E. Crooke, Oxford, 1925

TIMBERG, THOMAS A.: *The Marwaris: From Traders to Industrialists*, Vikas Publishing House, New Delhi, 1978

TOD, COL. JAMES: *Annals and antiquities of Rajasthan*, edited by W. Crooke (3 vols), Oxford University Press, 1920

WELCH, STUART CARY: *Imperial Mughal Painting*, George Braziller, New York, 1978

WILLS, C. H.: *A reply to the report on the Land-tenures and Special Powers of Certain Thikanedars of the Jaipur State.* Printed at I.M.H. Press, Delhi, 1891

WOODFORD, PEGGY: *Rise of the Raj*, Midas Books (Kent) and Humanities Press (New Jersey), 1978

WORSWICK, CLARK & EMBREE, AINSLEE: *The Last Empire – Photography in British India 1855–1911*, Gordon Fraser, London, 1976

Acknowledgements

IN JAIPUR we owe our thanks at Emerald House to the family of Khailshanker and Hemlata Durlabhji – in particular to Yogendra and Rashmikant; at Mandawa House to the family of Kanwar Devi Singh and Sajjan Kumari – in particular to Randhir and Manjul, Pradumn and Hemant; at Nawalgarh House to Kumar Sangram Singh, Sunny and Brigitte; at Bissau House to the late Thakur Chakrapani Singh and to May Singh; at Dundlod House to Thakur Rajvir Singh; and also to Kripal Singh Shekhawat, Dr A. K. Das, Bickram Dandiya, Raghuraj Kanwar, P. S. Rathore, Satya Prakash Sharma, K. G. Sharma, Rangi and Raghu Sinha.

In Shekhavati we extend our gratitude to Thakur Jai Singh of Mandawa, Rawal Madan Singh of Nawalgarh, Raja Sardar Singh of Khetri, Colonel Raghuvir Singh of Dundlod, N. K. Jhunjhunwala and V. S. Bhatnagar at Mukundgarh, Narpat Singh at Nawalgarh, Bal Krishan Johri at Ramgarh.

In New Delhi our thanks are owed to Yogesh Vaid, Rajeev Sethi, Geeta and Anuradha Kapur, L. N. Jhunjhunwala, G. D. Birla, Shanti Loke Nath, Gopal Dutia, Sunil Sethi, R. N. Sharma, Urvashi Butalia, Geeti Sen and B. K. Sharma; in London to Jacqueline and Louis Ridley, Mark Zebrowski, John Robert Alderman, Carolyn Eàrdley, Rosemary Vane-Wright and Mark Ritchie; and in Paris to Annik Wacziarg and Yves Vecquaud.

Our very special thanks go to Elwyn Blacker and Narendra Kumar without whom the book would not have been possible.